VOGUE®
KNITTING
VINTAGE
COLLECTION

VOGUE KNITTING

VINTAGE COLLECTION

Classic Knits from the 1930s-1960s

Edited by Trisha Malcolm

SOHO PUBLISHING COMPANY
NEW YORK

SOHO PUBLISHING COMPANY
233 Spring Street
New York, New York 10013

Editor-in-Chief
Trisha Malcolm

Editor
Annemarie McNamara

Art Director
Christine Lipert

Associate Art Director
Chi Ling Moy

Knitting Editors
Carla Patrick
Karen Greenwald

Technical Editor
Charlotte Parry

Managing Editor
Kathleen Kelly

Yarn Editors
Veronica Manno
Betty Christianson

Copy Editors
Suzie Elliott
Michelle Lo

Fashion Editor
Elenita Fabre

President and Publisher, SoHo Publishing Company
Art Joinnides

1 3 5 7 9 10 8 6 4 2

Library of Congress Cataloging-in-Publication Data
Vogue knitting vintage collection:classic knit patterns from the 1930s to1960s/edited by Trisha Malcolm
p.   cm.

ISBN:1-931543-00-3.
1. Knitting—Patterns. I. Title: Vintage collection. II Malcolm, Trisha, 1960-
TT820.V627 2001
746.43'20432-dc21   2001017041

Introduction

For over seventy years, knitters have looked to *Vogue Knitting* magazine for the latest knit fashions and clear instructions to create them. Many of the world's very best designers and technical experts have lent their talent to what most regard as the very best publication in its field. To celebrate our unique heritage, we've gathered together this one-of-a-kind collection of over thirty of the most popular *Vogue Knitting* patterns published between the 1930s and 1960s. Like us, readers will discover that these classic and timeless garments are just as appealing and chic today as when they originally appeared on the magazine pages. We've included clothing for babies, toddlers, and children, as well as sweaters and accessories for men and women in a wide range of styles. Now every member of the family has the opportunity to own and enjoy a piece of fashion history.

As early as the 1920s, fashion magazines like *Vogue* were publishing knitting patterns as a special feature. By the end of that decade, when the wave of postwar posterity had broken, an increasing number of cash-pressed women turned to knitting as a way to obtain fashionable sweaters at a reasonable cost. This marked the beginning of a knitting craze unprecedented in American history. People from all walks of life could be seen in leisure moments busily working with flying needles and balls of wool. To keep up with the rising demand for handknit patterns, the *Vogue Knitting Book*, a magazine devoted entirely to handknit patterns, was launched in 1932.

As the decade progressed, *Vogue* itself began increasingly adding articles on knit fashion and techniques to complement its steady supply of unbeatable patterns. In the Forties, when America went to war, *Vogue* rallied its forces, teaching readers how to unravel old woolens for reknitting and producing designs that were suitable for a variety of less-expensive yarns. In addition, the magazine encouraged knitters to work for charities, and helped organize clubs that would knit and then forward garments to war victims and fighters in need.

By the Fifties, matrimony and babies inspired more knitting than even wartime efforts. Viewed as synonymous with home and motherhood, knitting peaked in popularity. More and more young people began knitting, working nonstop on argyles and angoras to wear on high school and college campuses. As knitting drew more enthusiasts, magazines such as *Vogue Knitting* and *Woman's Day* committed more pages to knitting patterns. In addition to argyle anything, cashmere pullovers were popular, as were shoulder warmers (or "shrugs"), which many liked to wear over their evening gowns.

The Sixties brought with it a new trend called "quick knitting"—jumbo stitches made with giant needles and multiple strands of yarn. Ideal for busy, modern women who had little time but loved to knit, big-needle patterns offered chunky-chic styles with simple silhouettes ideal for slipping over a mod bodystocking or skirt. By the 1970s, knitting had begun to decidedly decline in popularity. Even so, great knitting publications, like Barbara Walker's stitch dictionaries and Elizabeth Zimmermann's masterpiece, *Knitting Without Tears*, kept the faithful delighted and many newcomers intrigued.

Today, knitting has regained and even surpassed its previous popularity. More and more people are learning to knit, and an increasing number of world-class designers are lending their talents to the craft. Likewise, a distinct nostalgia for classic designs from years past has surfaced—designs that are now revived and rejuvenated with contemporary yarns, modern materials, and cutting-edge techniques.

While fashion, as life, has changed throughout the years, knitting has prevailed. Whether for economy or relaxation, knitting has been delighting and rewarding practitioners for decades. We hope you enjoy this walk down memory lane, and these wonderful, timeless fashions we've updated for you to knit today.

Table of Contents

Before You Begin

This book was designed as an anthology of patterns. For more precise technical explanation, refer to Vogue Knitting—The Ultimate Knitting Book (New York: Pantheon Books).

YARN SELECTION

Some of the yarns, or colors, used in the original designer patterns are no longer available. We have provided substitute yarns readily available in the U.S. and Canada at the time of printing. The Resources page lists addresses of yarn distributors—contact them for the name of a retailer in your area or for mail-order information.

If you wish to substitute a yarn, check the gauge carefully to ensure the finished garment will knit to the correct measurements. To facilitate yarn substitution, Vogue Knitting grades yarn by the standard stitch gauge obtained in stockinette stitch. There is a grading number in the Materials section of each pattern. Look for a substitute yarn that falls into the same category—the suggested gauge on the ball band should be comparable to that on the Yarn Symbols Chart (right).

After successfully gauge-swatching in a substitute yarn, you'll need to determine yarn requirements. First, find the total length of the original yarn in the pattern (multiply number of balls by yards/meters per ball). Divide this figure by the new yards/meters per ball (listed on the ball band). Round up to the next whole number. The answer is the number of balls required.

GAUGE

To ensure a successful project, always knit a gauge swatch before beginning . Normally, gauge is measured over a four-inch (10cm) square. Using the needles and yarn suggested, cast on enough stitches to knit a square at least this size.

Gauge is usually given in stockinette stitch, but if the pattern calls for a specific stitch, work this stitch for the swatch. Measure stitches carefully with a ruler or gauge tool. If the swatch is smaller than the stated gauge (more stitches per inch/cm), try larger needles. If it is larger (fewer stitches per inch/cm), use smaller needles. Before proceeding, experiment with needle size until the gauge exactly matches the one given.

If a pattern calls for knitting in the round, it may tighten the gauge, so if the gauge was measured on a flat swatch, take another reading after beginning the project.

READING PATTERNS

Each pattern is rated for technical ability. Choose a pattern that fits within your experience range. Read all instructions thoroughly before starting to knit a gauge swatch and again before beginning a project. Familiarize yourself with all abbreviations (see Knitting Terms and Abbreviations, opposite). Refer to the Vogue Knitting book for clear explanations of any stitches or techniques you may not be familiar with.

Generally, patterns are written in several sizes. The smallest appears first, and figures for larger sizes are given in parentheses. Where only one figure appears, it applies to all sizes. Highlight numbers pertaining to your size before beginning.

Knitted measurements are the dimensions of the garment after all the pieces have been sewn together. Usually, three measurements are given: finished chest; finished length; and sleeve width at upper arm. The finished chest measurement is the width around the entire sweater at the underarm. For cardigans, the width is determined with the front bands buttoned. Finished length is measured from the highest point of the shoulder to the bottom of the ribbing. Sleeve width is measured at the upper arm, after all increases have been worked and before any cap shaping takes place.

Schematics are a valuable tool for determining size selection and proper fit. Schematics are scale drawings showing the dimensions of the finished knitted pieces.

Work figures given inside brackets the number of times stated afterward. Directions immediately following an asterisk are to be repeated the given number of times. If the instructions call for working even, work in the same pattern stitch without increasing or decreasing.

YARN SYMBOLS

The following numbers 1-6 represent a range of stitch gauges. Note that these numbers correspond to the standard gauge in stockinette stitch.

1 FINE WEIGHT
(29-32 stitches per 4"/10cm)
Includes baby and fingering yarns, and some of the heavier crochet cottons.

2 LIGHTWEIGHT
(25-28 stitches per 4"/10cm)
Includes sport yarn, sock yarn, UK 4-ply and lightweight DK yarns.

3 MEDIUM WEIGHT
(21-24 stitches per 4"/10cm)
Includes DK and worsted, the most commonly used knitting yarns.

4 MEDIUM-HEAVY WEIGHT
(17-20 stitches per 4"/10cm)
Also called heavy worsted or Aran.

5 BULKY WEIGHT
(13-16 stitches per 4"/10cm)
Also called chunky. Includes heavier Icelandic yarns.

6 EXTRA-BULKY WEIGHT
(9-12 stitches per 4"/10cm)
The heaviest yarns available.

KNITTING TERMS AND ABBREVIATIONS

approx approximately

beg begin(ning)

bind off Used to finish an edge and keep stitches from unraveling. Lift the first stitch over the second, the second over the third, etc. (UK: cast off)

cast on A foundation row of stitches placed on the needle in order to begin knitting.

CC contrast color

ch chain(s)

cm centimeter(s)

cont continue(ing)

dc double crochet (UK: tr-treble)

dec decrease(ing)—Reduce the stitches in a row (knit 2 together).

dpn double-pointed needle(s)

foll follow(s)(ing)

g gram(s)

garter stitch Knit every row. Circular knitting: knit one round, then purl one round.

hdc half-double crochet (UK: htr-half treble)

inc increase(ing)—Add stitches in a row (knit into the front and back of a stitch).

k knit

k2tog knit 2 stitches together

lp(s) loops(s)

LH left hand

m meter(s)

M1 make one stitch—With the needle tip, lift the strand between the last stitch worked and next stitch on the left-hand needle and knit into the back of it. One stitch has been added.

MC main color

mm millimeter(s)

oz ounce(s)

p purl

p2tog purl 2 stitches together

pat pattern

pick up and knit (purl) Knit (or purl) into the loops along an edge.

pm place markers—Place or attach a loop of contrast yarn or purchased stitch marker as indicated.

psso pass slip stitch over

rem remain(s)(ing)

rep repeat

rev St st reverse Stockinette stitch—Purl right-side rows, knit wrong-side rows. Circular knitting: purl all rounds. (UK: reverse stocking stitch)

rnd(s) round(s)

RH right hand

RS right side(s)

sc single crochet (UK: dc - double crochet)

sk skip

SKP Slip 1, knit 1, pass slip stitch over knit 1

sl slip—An unworked stitch made by passing a stitch from the left-hand to the right-hand needle as if to purl.

sl st slip stitch (UK: single crochet)

ssk slip, slip, knit—Slip next 2 stitches knitwise, one at a time, to right-hand needle. Insert tip of left-hand needle into fronts of these stitches from left to right. Knit them together. One stitch has been decreased.

st(s) stitch(es)

St st Stockinette stitch—Knit right-side rows, purl wrong-side rows. Circular knitting: knit all rounds. (UK: stocking stitch)

tbl through back of loop

tog together

WS wrong side(s)

wyif with yarn in front

wyib with yarn in back

work even Continue in pattern without increasing or decreasing. (UK: work straight)

yd yard(s)

yo yarn over—Make a new stitch by wrapping the yarn over the right-hand needle. (UK: yfwd, yon, yrn)

* repeat directions following * as many times as indicated.

[ ] Repeat directions inside brackets as many times as indicated.

FOLLOWING CHARTS

Charts are a convenient way to follow colorwork, lace, cable, and other stitch patterns. *Vogue Knitting* stitch charts utilize the universal language of "symbolcraft." Each symbolcraft symbol represents the stitch as it appears on the right side of the work. For example, the symbol for the knit stitch is a vertical line and the symbol for a purl stitch is a horizontal one. On right-side rows, work the stitches as they appear on the chart—knitting the vertical lines and purling the horizontal ones. When reading wrong-side rows, work the opposite of what is shown; that is, purl the vertical lines and knit the horizontal ones.

Each square on a chart represents one stitch and each horizontal row of squares equals a row or round. When knitting back and forth on straight needles, right-side rows (RS) are read right to left, wrong-side rows (WS) are read from left to right, bottom to top. When knitting in rounds on circular needles, read charts from right to left on every round, repeating any stitch and row repeats as directed in the pattern. Posting a self-adhesive note under the working row is an easy way to keep track on a chart.

Sometimes, only a single repeat of the pattern is charted. Heavy lines drawn through the entire chart indicate a repeat. The lines are the equivalent of an asterisk (*) or brackets [] used in written instructions.

KNITTING NEEDLES		
US	METRIC	UK
0	2mm	14
1	2.25mm	13
	2.5mm	
2	2.75mm	12
	3mm	11
3	3.25mm	10
4	3.5mm	
5	3.75mm	9
	4mm	8
6		
7	4.5mm	7
8	5mm	6
9	5mm	5
10	6mm	4
10½	6.5mm	3
	7mm	2
	7.5mm	1
11	8mm	0
13	9mm	00
15	10mm	000

Women's Spring/Summer

Spring and summer knits from the past reflect the enduring interest in lighter garments. From brightly patterned pullovers to elegant tailored tops, these warm weather fashions will stand the test of time.

The neat, clean look of a silk blouse...as fresh today as it was years ago. The ribs of this back-buttoning stunner rise to a textured, eyelet stitch yoke, with short, set-in sleeves and Peter Pan collar. Shown in size 34. The Short-Sleeved Silk Top first appeared in the July 1946 issue of the original Vogue Knitting magazine.

Short-Sleeved Silk Top

FOR INTERMEDIATE KNITTERS

SIZES
To fit 30 (32, 34, 36, 38)"/76 (81, 86, 91, 96)cm bust. Directions are for smallest size with larger sizes in parentheses. If there is only one figure, it applies to all sizes.

KNITTED MEASUREMENTS
● Bust at underarm 31 (33½, 35, 38, 39)"/77 (84, 87, 94, 98)cm.
● Length 21 (21½, 22, 22½, 23)"/52.5 (54, 55.5, 56.5, 57.5)cm.
● Upper arm 11 (11¾, 11¾, 12½, 12½)"/28 (29.5, 29.5, 31.5, 31.5)cm.

MATERIALS
Original Yarn
● 8 (9, 9, 10, 11) 1½oz/40g balls (each approx 160yds/147m) of Schaffhauser/Skacel Imports *Silk* (silk 2) in #08 celery
Substitute Yarn
● 7 (8, 8, 8, 9) 1¾oz/50g balls (each approx 201yds/186m) of Jaeger Handknits *Silk 4 Ply* (silk 2) in #130 ivory
● One pair size 2 (2.5mm) needles OR SIZE TO OBTAIN GAUGE
● Size C/2 (2.5mm) crochet hook
● Four ⁷⁄₁₆"/11mm buttons

Note
The original yarn used for this sweater is no longer available. A comparable substitution has been made, which is

available at the time of printing. Check gauge of substitute yarns very carefully before beginning.

GAUGES
● 35 sts and 38 rows to 4"/10cm over k3, p3 rib (slightly stretched) using size 2 (2.5mm) needles.
● 34 sts and 40 rows to 4"/10cm over pat st using size 2 (2.5mm) needles. FOR PERFECT FIT, TAKE TIME TO CHECK GAUGES.

Note
Follow either written or chart instructions for pat st.

STITCH GLOSSARY
Pat St (multiple of 6 sts + 3)
Row 1 (RS) *Yo, sl next 2 sts tog knit-wise, k1, pass 2 sl sts over k1 (S2KP), yo, p3; rep from *, end yo, S2KP, yo.
Row 2 Knit.
Rows 3 and 5 *K3, p3; rep from *, end k3.
Rows 4 and 6 P3, *k3, p3; rep from * to end. Rep rows 1-6 for pat st.

BACK
With size 2 (2.5mm) needles, cast on 111 (123, 129, 141, 147) sts.
Beg rib: Row 1 (RS) *K3, p3; rep from *, end k3.
Row 2 K the knit sts and p the purl sts. Rep rows 1 and 2 for rib for 3"/7.5cm. Cont in rib, inc 1 st each side (working inc sts into rib) on next row and rep inc every 6th row 3 (3, 0, 0, 0) times, every

8th row 8 (8, 11, 11, 9) times, every 10th row 0 (0, 0, 0, 2) times—135 (147, 153, 165, 171) sts. Work even in rib until piece measures 12½ (12½, 13, 13, 13½)"/31 (31, 32.5, 32.5, 33.5)cm from beg.

Armhole shaping
Bind off 4 sts at beg of next 0 (2, 2, 2, 2) rows, 3 sts at beg of next 2 rows, 2 sts at beg of next 4 (2, 2, 2, 2) rows. Dec 1 st each side every other row 2 (1, 1, 2, 2) times—117 (127, 133, 143, 149) sts.
Beg pat st: Row 1 (RS) P3 (2, 2, 1, 1), work pat st to last 3 (2, 2, 1, 1) sts, p to end. Cont in pat st, working 3 (2, 2, 1, 1) sts each side in rev St st (p on RS, k on WS), until armhole measures 3½ (4, 4, 4½, 4½)"/9 (10.5, 10.5, 11.5, 11.5)cm, end with a WS row.

Back opening
Next row (RS) Work 58 (63, 66, 71, 74) sts, join 2nd ball of yarn and bind off center st, work to end. Work both sides at once until armhole measures 7½ (8, 8, 8½, 8½)"/19 (20.5, 20.5, 21.5, 21.5)cm.

Shoulder shaping
Bind off from each shoulder edge 6 (7, 8, 9, 10) sts twice, 7 (8, 8, 9, 9) sts twice, 7 (8, 9, 8, 9) sts once. Bind off rem 25 (25, 25, 27, 27) sts each side.

FRONT
Work as for back, omitting back opening, until armhole measures 5½ (6, 6, 6½, 6½)"/14 (15.5, 15.5, 16.5, 16.5)cm.

Neck and shoulder shaping

Next row (RS) Work 51 (56, 59, 62, 65) sts, join 2nd ball of yarn and bind off 15 (15, 15, 19, 19) sts, work to end. Working both sides at once, bind off from each neck edge 3 sts twice, 2 sts twice, dec 1 st every other row 8 times, AT SAME TIME, when same length as back to shoulder, work shoulder shaping as for back.

SLEEVES

With size 2 (2.5mm) needles, cast on 95 (101, 101, 107, 107) sts.
Beg pat st: Row 1 (RS) P1, work pat st to last st, p1. Cont in pat st, working first and last st in rev St st, until piece measures 4½ (4½, 4½, 5, 5)"/11.5 (11.5, 11.5, 12.5, 12.5)cm from beg, end with a WS row.

Cap shaping

Bind off 4 sts at beg of next 2 rows, 3 sts at beg of next 2 rows, 2 sts at beg of next 2 rows. Dec 1 st each side every other row 15 (17, 17, 19, 19) times, every row 12 (12, 12, 14, 14) times. Bind off rem 23 (25, 25, 23, 23) sts.

FINISHING

Block pieces. Sew shoulder seams.

Collar (make 2 pieces)
With size 2 (2.5mm) needles, cast on 67 (67, 67, 73, 73) sts.
Beg pat st: Row 1 (RS) K2 (garter st edge), work pat st to last 2 sts, k2 (garter st edge). Cont in pat st, keeping 2 sts each side in garter st (k every row) until piece measures 2"/5cm. Bind off. With RS facing and crochet hook, work 1 row of sc around back opening. Place markers on left back edge for 4 button loops, the first one at top edge, the last one at lower edge, and 2 others evenly between. Work 1 more row of sc, working button loops at markers by ch 6, sk 1 sc for each button loop. Sew cast-on edge of one collar piece invisibly from RS around one-half of neck, beg at center front neck and ending at back neck opening. Sew other piece on other side of neck. Set in sleeves. Sew side and sleeve seams. Sew on buttons.

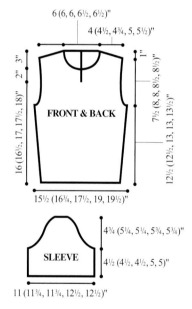

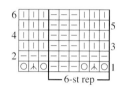

6-st rep

Stitch Key

☐ K on RS, p on WS

☐ P on RS, k on WS

○ Yarn over

⅄ S2kp

Tailored Seed-Stitch Top

This summer's answer to the suit! This short-sleeved, seed-stitch sweater is tailored to fit with fold-back sleeve cuffs, a back-buttoned belt, and a contrasting running stitch trim. Pair it with classic pants or go for the clean lines of a fitted skirt. Shown in size Small. The Tailored Seed-Stitch Top first appeared in The 3rd Book of Vogue Knitting published in the 1930s.

Tailored Seed-Stitch Top

FOR INTERMEDIATE KNITTERS

SIZES
To fit X-Small (Small, Medium, Large). Directions are for smallest size with larger sizes in parentheses. If there is only one figure, it applies to all sizes.

KNITTED MEASUREMENTS
● Bust at underarm (buttoned) 35 (37, 39, 41)"/89 (94, 99, 104)cm.
● Length 18 (18½, 19½, 20)"/46 (47, 49.5, 51)cm.
● Upper arm 15 (16, 17, 18)"/38 (41, 43, 46)cm.

MATERIALS
Original Yarn
● 9 (10, 10, 11) 1¾oz/50g balls (each approx 181yds/166m) of Hayfield/Cascade *Cotton Classics 4 ply* (cotton 2) in #073022 navy (MC)
● I ball in #073001 natural (CC)
Substitute Yarn
● 9 (10, 10, 11) 1¾oz/50g balls (each approx 186yds/170m) of Rowan Yarns *4 Ply Cotton* (cotton 2) in #102 marine (navy) (MC)
● 1 ball in #113 bleached (white) (CC)
● One pair size 3 (3mm) needles OR SIZE TO OBTAIN GAUGE
● Stitch holders and markers
● Tapestry needle
● Six ¾"/20mm buttons

Note
The original yarn used for this sweater is no longer available. A comparable substitution has been made, which is available at the time of printing. Check gauge of substitute yarns very carefully before beginning.

GAUGE
28 sts and 44 rows to 4"/10cm over seed st using size 3 (3mm) needles. FOR PERFECT FIT, TAKE TIME TO CHECK GAUGE.

STITCH GLOSSARY
Seed Stitch
Row 1(RS) *K1, p1; rep from * to end.
Row 2 K the purl sts and p the knit sts. Rep row 2 for seed st.

BACK
With MC, cast on 98 (102, 106, 112) sts. Beg with row 1, work in seed st for 3"/7.5cm, end with a WS row. Cont in pat, AT SAME TIME, inc 1 st each side (working inc sts into pat) every 6th row 5 (6, 6, 6) times, every 8th row 4 (4, 6, 6) times—116 (122, 130, 136) sts. Work even until piece measures 9½ (9½, 10, 10)"/24 (24, 25.5, 25.5)cm from beg, end with a WS row.

Armhole shaping
Bind off 6 sts at beg of next 2 rows. Dec 1 st each edge every other row 5 (5, 6, 6) times—94 (100, 106, 112) sts. Work even until armhole measures 7½

(8, 8½, 9)"/19 (20.5, 21.5, 23)cm, end with a WS row.

Shoulder shaping
Bind off 7 (7, 8, 8) sts at beg of next 6 rows, 5 (7, 6, 8) sts at beg of next 2 rows. Bind off rem 42 (44, 46, 48) sts.

Pocket lining (make 1)
With MC, cast on 24 sts and work in St st for 2½"/6.5cm. Sl sts to holder.

LEFT FRONT
With MC, cast on 3 sts. Work row 1 of seed st pat. Cont in pat, AT SAME TIME, inc 1 st each side (working inc sts into pat) every row 19 (20, 21, 21) times—41 (43, 45, 45) sts.
Next row (RS) Cast on 6 sts (side edge), work in pat to end—47 (49, 51, 51) sts.
Next row Cast on 11 sts (facing), p same 11 sts, place marker (pm), work in pat to end—58 (60, 62, 62) sts.
Next row (RS) Cast on 7 sts, work to marker, sl 1, k10—65 (67, 69, 69) sts. Work even until piece measures 3"/7.5cm along side edge. Cont in pat, AT SAME TIME, inc 1 st at side edge every other row 2 (4, 6, 8) times, then every 4th row 14 times—81 (85, 89, 91) sts. Work even until piece measures same as back to underarm, end with a WS row.

Armhole shaping
Next row (RS) Bind off 6 sts, work to marker, sl 1, beg with row 1, work seed

st pat on 10 sts—75 (79, 83, 85) sts.
Next row (WS) Inc 1 in first st, work in pat to st before marker, p1, work to end—76 (80, 84, 86) sts. Shape facing and armhole simultaneously as foll: Dec 1 st at armhole edge every other row 6 times, AT SAME TIME, inc 1 st at facing edge (working inc sts into seed st) every row 22 (24, 26, 26) times—92 (98, 104, 106) sts. When armhole measures 2½"/6.5cm, end with a WS row.

Pocket joining
Next row (RS) Work 12 (14, 16, 18) sts, place next 24 sts on holder (pocket opening), with k side facing, k 24 sts of pocket lining from holder, work to end. Cont to shape facing and then work even until armhole measures same as back, end with a WS row.

Shoulder and neck shaping
Next row (RS) Bind off 7 (7, 8, 8) sts, work to end.
Next row (WS) Work 14 (16, 18, 18) sts, join 2nd ball of yarn and bind off 38 sts, work to end. Cont to shape shoulders as for back, AT SAME TIME, bind off at each neck edge 4 sts twice, 3 (4, 5, 5) sts twice. Place 5 markers for buttons, first 1"/2.5cm from beg of facing and 4 others approx 2"/5cm apart.

RIGHT FRONT
Work right front to correspond to left front, reversing shaping and omitting pocket opening. Make buttonholes opposite markers at beg of RS rows as foll: Work 2 sts, bind off 4 sts, work 3 sts, sl 1, work 4 sts, bind off 4 sts, work to end. On next row, cast on 4

sts over each set of bound-off sts of previous row.

SLEEVES
With MC, cast on 81 (84, 88, 92) sts. Beg with a k row, work 5 rows in St st.
Next row (WS) Knit (turning ridge). Beg with row 1, work in seed st for 2"/5cm, AT SAME TIME, dec 1 st each side every 6th row twice, end with a RS row—77 (80, 84, 88) sts. K 2 rows for turning ridge.
Next row (RS) Work row 1 of seed st and mark row for RS of sleeve. Work even for 1"/2.5cm. Cont in pat, AT SAME TIME, inc 1 st each side every other row 0 (0, 2, 3) times, every 4th row 11 (16, 16, 16) times, every 6th row 3 (0, 0, 0) times—105 (112, 120, 126) sts. Work even until piece measures 7"/18cm from turning ridge, end with a WS row.

Cap shaping
Bind off 3 sts at beg of next 25 rows. Bind off 2 (2, 3, 3) sts at beg of next 10 rows. Bind off rem 10 (17, 15, 21) sts.

FINISHING
Block pieces. With RS facing and MC, k24 sts from holder on left front. K 1 row and bind off at same time. Sew shoulder seams. Set in sleeves. Sew side and sleeve seams. Fold cuff at first turning ridge (k side faces you) and sew in place. Turn cuff at 2nd turning ridge to RS of sleeve and tack in place. Blind st front facings to WS. With MC, work buttonhole st around buttonholes.

Collar
With MC, cast on 84 (89, 94, 99) sts. Beg with row 1, work in seed st for 2¼"/6cm. K 1 row (turning ridge). Beg

with a k row, cont in St st until piece is 2½"/6.5cm from turning ridge. Bind off. With seed st as RS, fold collar in half lengthwise at turning ridge and pin to center back neck. Pin ends of collar 2 ½"/6.5cm from front lapel edges. Easing to fit, sew seed st edge of collar to inside of neck and St st edge to RS of sweater.

Belt
(Note: Belt is made in 2 sections to fit across back of sweater.) With MC, cast on 47 (49, 51, 53) sts. Beg with row 1, work 16 rows in seed st. P 2 rows (turning ridge). Beg with a k row, work 14 rows in St st. Bind off. With MC, cast on 44 (46, 48, 51) sts. Beg with row 1, work seed st to end, inc 1 in last st. Cont in pat, AT SAME TIME, inc 1 st at same edge every row 6 times. Work 2 rows even. Dec 1 st at same edge every row 7 times.
Next row (RS) Purl (turning ridge).
Next row (WS) Inc 1 st in first st, purl to end. Cont in St st, inc 1 st at same edge every row 6 times. Cont in pat, work 2 rows even, then dec 1 st at same edge every row 7 times. Bind off. Fold pieces in half at turning ridge and sew open edges. With seed st as RS, sew straight end of pointed piece to waistline at right side seam. Sew 2nd belt to opposite seam to match. Adjust for size and sew button to secure pointed piece on top of straight piece.

Running st
With 2 strands of CC held tog and tapestry needle, embroider running st around front and lapel edges, collar, top edge of cuffs and lower edges of front and back.

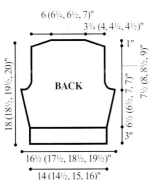

BACK

6 (6¼, 6½, 7)"
3¾ (4, 4¼, 4½)"
1"
18 (18½, 19½, 20)"
7½ (8, 8½, 9)"
6½ (6½, 7, 7)"
3"
16½ (17½, 18½, 19½)"
14 (14½, 15, 16)"

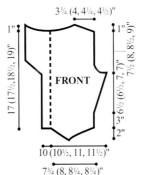

FRONT

3¾ (4, 4¼, 4½)"
1"
1"
1"
9"
17 (17½, 18½, 19)"
7½ (8, 8½, 9)"
6½ (6½, 7, 7)"
3"
2"
10 (10½, 11, 11½)"
7¾ (8, 8¼, 8¼)"

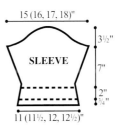

SLEEVE

15 (16, 17, 18)"
3½"
7"
2"
¾"
11 (11½, 12, 12½)"

Photo: Leombruno-Bodi

The crisp, clean elegance of white linen… Back in 1963, this diamond-and-braid patterned shell with rolled-edges debuted in natural linen. Today, we've updated the color and the yarn to a thoroughly modern linen-blend. Shown in size Small. The Sleeveless Linen Top first appeared in the Spring/Summer 1963 issue of the original Vogue Knitting magazine.

Sleeveless Linen Top

FOR INTERMEDIATE KNITTERS

SIZES
To fit X-Small (Small, Medium, Large, X-Large). Directions are for smallest size with larger sizes in parentheses. If there is only one figure, it applies to all sizes.

KNITTED MEASUREMENTS
● Bust 32½ (33½, 35, 37, 38)"/82.5 (85, 89, 94, 96.5)cm.
● Length 21½"/54.5cm.

MATERIALS
Original Yarn
● (4, 5, 5, 6) 3½oz/100g balls (each approx 163yds/150m) of Tahki Yarns *Laguna 2000* (viscose/linen 3) in #6401 white
Substitute Yarn
● 6 (6, 7, 7, 9) 1¾oz/50g balls (each approx 122yds/111m) of Naturally/ S.R. Kertzer, Ltd. *Cotton Connection D.K. No. 3* (cotton/linen 3) in #03 natural
● One pair each sizes 5 and 6 (3.75 and 4mm) needles OR SIZE TO OBTAIN GAUGE
● Size E/4 (3.5mm) crochet hook
● Cable needle
● Two ½"/13mm buttons

Note
The original yarn used for this sweater is no longer available. A comparable substitution has been made, which is available at the time of printing. Check gauge of substitute yarns very carefully before beginning.

GAUGE
24 sts and 28 rows to 4"/10cm across all pat sts using size 6 (4mm) needles. FOR PERFECT FIT, TAKE TIME TO CHECK GAUGE.

STITCH GLOSSARY
4-st RPC
Sl 3 sts to cn and hold to *back,* k1, k3 from cn.
4-st LPC
Sl 1 st to cn and hold to *front,* k3, k1 from cn.
2-st RPC
Sl 1 st to cn and hold to *back,* k next st tbl, p1 from cn.
2-st LPC
Sl 1 st to cn and hold to *front,* p next st, k1 tbl from cn.
1/2 LPC
Sl 2 sts to cn and hold to *front,* k1, k first st from cn, then p 2nd st.

Seed Stitch
Row 1 (RS) *K1, p1; rep from * to end.
Row 2 *K the purl sts and p the knit sts. Rep row 2 for seed st.

BACK
With smaller needles, cast on 88 (90, 94, 98, 102) sts. Work in seed st for 1"/2.5cm. P next row on WS, inc 10 (11, 10, 12, 13) sts evenly spaced—98 (101, 104, 110, 115) sts. Change to larger needles.

Beg pats
Row 1 (RS) P8 (9, 10, 11, 13) for reverse St st, work 9 sts double cable pat, p3 (3, 3, 4, 4), 13 sts in diamond pat, p3 (3, 3, 4, 4), 9 sts in double cable pat, p8 (9, 10, 10, 11), 9 sts in double cable pat, p3 (3, 3, 4, 4), 13 sts in diamond pat, p3 (3, 3, 4, 4), 9 sts in double cable pat, p8 (9, 10, 11, 13) for reverse St st. Cont in pats as established, with sts between chart pats in reverse St st, until piece measures 13½ (13, 13, 12¾, 12½)"/34 (33, 33, 32.5, 32)cm from beg.

Armhole shaping
Bind off 3 (3, 4, 4, 4) sts at beg of next 2 rows, 2 sts at beg of next 2 (2, 2, 2, 4) rows, dec 1 st each side every other row 2 (3, 3, 4, 4) times—84 (85, 86, 90, 91) sts. Work even in pats until armhole measures 3 (3½, 3½, 3¾, 4)"/7.5 (9, 9, 9.5, 10)cm.

Back neck opening
Next row (RS) Work 41 (41, 42, 44, 44) sts, join 2nd ball of yarn and bind off center 2 (3, 2, 2, 3) sts, work to end. Work both sides at once until armhole measures 7 (7½, 7½, 7¾, 8)"/18 (19, 19, 19.5, 20.5)cm.

Shoulder shaping
Bind off from each shoulder edge 6 sts 4 (4, 4, 2, 2) times, 7 sts 0 (0, 0, 2, 2) times. Bind off rem 17 (17, 18, 18, 18) sts each side for neck.

FRONT

Work as for back omitting neck opening and work until armhole measures 5½ (6, 6, 6¼, 6½)"/14 (15, 15, 16, 16.5)cm.

Neck shaping

Next row (RS) Work 34 (34, 34, 36, 36) sts, join 2nd ball of yarn and bind off center 16 (17, 18, 18, 19) sts, work to end. Working both sides at once, bind off 3 sts from each neck edge once, 2 sts twice, then dec 1 st every other row 3 times—24 (24, 24, 26, 26) sts rem each side. When same length as back, shape shoulders as for back.

FINISHING

Block pieces to measurements. Sew shoulder seams. With smaller needles, pick up and k 63 (68, 68, 70, 72) sts evenly around armholes. P 1 row on WS, then p 1 row, k 1 row, p 1 row. Bind off knitwise (band will roll to inside). With smaller needles, pick up and knit 70 (70, 74, 74, 74) sts evenly

around neck edge. Work as for armhole band. With smaller needles, pick up and k 22 sts along right back opening, 2 (3, 2, 2, 3) sts at center, other side of opening to correspond. P 1 row on WS, then p next row.

Next row (WS) K to 1 st before center 2 (3, 2, 2, 3) sts, k2tog, k 0 (1, 0, 0, 1), k2tog, k to end. Bind off purlwise. Work 2 ch-8 loops and fasten securely under left back rolled edge spaced evenly. Sew on buttons opposite loops. Sew side seams.

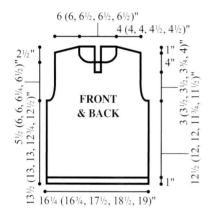

6 (6, 6½, 6½, 6½)"
4 (4, 4, 4½, 4½)"
2½"
1"
4"
5½ (6, 6, 6¼, 6½)"
3 (3½, 3½, 3¾, 4)"
13½ (13, 13, 12¾, 12½)"
12½ (12, 12, 11¾, 11½)"
1"

FRONT & BACK

16¼ (16¾, 17½, 18½, 19)"

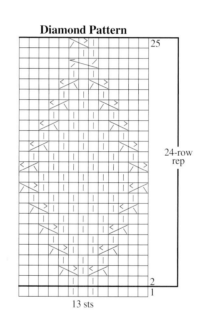

Diamond Pattern

25

24-row rep

2
1

13 sts

Double Cable Pattern

6

1

9 sts

Stitch Key

K on RS, p on WS

P on RS, k on WS

4-st RPC

4-st LPC

2-st RPC

2-st LPC

1/2 LPC

Summer-Style Aran Pullover

This breezy Aran pullover sports jaunty tassels just like the original. The oversized sweater is hemmed along the neck and edges and features set-in, three-quarter sleeves. Shown in size Medium. The Summer-Style Aran Pullover first appeared in the Spring/Summer 1961 issue of the original *Vogue Knitting* magazine.

Photo: Leombruno-Bodi

Summer-Style Aran Pullover

FOR INTERMEDIATE KNITTERS

SIZES
To fit Petite or X-Small (Small, Medium, Large). Directions are for smallest size with larger sizes in parentheses. If there is only one figure, it applies to all sizes.

KNITTED MEASUREMENTS
● Bust at underarm 37 (38½, 41, 43)"/94 (98, 104, 109)cm.
● Length 21½ (21¾, 22½, 22¾)"/54.5 (55, 57, 58)cm.
● Upper arm 13¼ (14, 14½, 15)"/33.5 (35.5, 37, 38)cm.

MATERIALS
Original Yarn
● 8 (8, 9, 10) 3½oz/100g balls (each approx 145yds/130m) of Bernat/Spinrite *Gloucester* (cotton 4) in #5342 white
Substitute Yarn
● 14 (15, 16, 18) 1¾oz/50g balls (each approx 82yds/75m) of Garnstudio/Aurora Yarns *Paris* (cotton 4) in #16 white
● One pair each sizes 7 and 9 (4.5 and 5.5mm) needles OR SIZE TO OBTAIN GAUGE
● Size 7 (4.5mm) circular needle, 24"/60cm long
● Cable needle (cn)
● Size G (4.5mm) crochet hook

Note
The original yarn used for this sweater is no longer available. A comparable substitution has been made, which is available at the time of printing. Check gauge of substitute yarns very carefully before beginning.

GAUGES
● 18 sts and 24 rows to 4"/10cm over St st using size 7 (4.5mm) needles.
● 19 sts and 23 rows to 4"/10cm over chart pat using size 9 (5.5mm) needles. FOR PERFECT FIT, TAKE TIME TO CHECK GAUGES.

STITCH GLOSSARY
Make Bobble (MB)
In next st, [k1 in front lp, k1 in back lp] twice, k1 in front lp—5 sts made. Turn, p2tog, p1, p2tog, turn, SK2P.
3-st Back Purl Cross
Sl 1 st to cn and hold to *back* of work, k2, p1 from cn.
3-st Front Purl Cross
Sl 2 sts to cn and hold to *front* of work, p1, k2 from cn.
4-st Back Cross
Sl 2 sts to cn and hold to *back* of work, k2, k2 from cn.
5-st Cable
Sl 3 sts to cn and hold to *back* of work, k2; p1, k2 from cn.

BACK
With smaller needles, cast on 83 (85, 91, 95) sts. Work in St st (k on RS, p on WS)

for 1"/2.5cm, end with a RS row. K 1 row (turning ridge). Cont in St st for 1"/2.5cm above turning ridge, inc 4 (6, 6, 6) sts evenly across last WS row—87 (91, 97, 101) sts. Change to larger needles.
Beg chart pat: Row 1 (RS) K2 (4, 7, 9) sts, work 29-st rep of chart twice, then sts 1-25 once, k2 (4, 7, 9) sts. Cont to work rows 1-24 of chart pat 3 times, keeping first and last sts in St st and center 83 sts in chart pat, AT SAME TIME, when piece measures 12½ (12½, 13, 13)"/32 (32, 33, 33)cm above turning ridge, end with a WS row.

Armhole shaping
Bind off 7 sts at beg of next 2 rows. Dec 1 st each side every other row 3 (3, 4, 4) times—67 (71, 75, 79) sts. After 3rd rep of chart pat is complete, work rows 1-2 once. Change to smaller needles.
Next row (RS) Work in St st, dec 4 sts evenly across—63 (67, 71, 75) sts. Cont to work in St st until armhole measures 7¼ (7½, 7¾, 8)"/18.5 (19, 19.5, 20.5)cm, end with a WS row.

Neck and shoulder shaping
Next row (RS) K18 (19, 20, 21) sts, join 2nd ball of yarn and bind off 27 (29, 31, 33) sts, work to end. Working both sides at once, bind off 3 sts from each neck edge 3 times, AT SAME TIME, when armhole measures 8¼ (8½, 8¾, 9)"/21 (21.5, 22, 23)cm, bind off from each armhole edge 4 (5, 5, 6) sts once, then 5 (5, 6, 6) sts once.

FRONT

Work as for back.

SLEEVES

With smaller needles, cast on 48 (51, 53, 56) sts. Work in St st for 1"/2.5cm, end with a RS row. K 1 row (turning ridge). Cont in St st, inc 1 st each side every 12th row 6 times—60 (63, 65, 68) sts. Work even until piece measures 14 (14, 14½, 14½)"/35.5 (35.5, 37, 37)cm from beg, end with a WS row.

Cap shaping

Bind off 6 sts at beg of next 2 rows. Dec 1 st each side every other row 12 (13, 14, 15) times, then bind off 2 sts at beg of next 6 rows. Bind off rem 12 (13, 13, 14) sts.

FINISHING

Block pieces. Sew shoulder seams.

Neck facing

With RS facing and circular needle, pick up and k107 (111, 115, 119) sts evenly around neck edge. Join.
Next rnd Purl (turning ridge). Cont to work in St st (k every rnd) until piece measures 1"/2.5cm from turning ridge. Bind off loosely. Fold neck facing to WS at turning ridge and sew in place. Set in sleeves. Sew side and sleeve seams. Fold hem and cuffs to WS at turning ridge and sew in place.

Tassels

Make 4 tassels, 2"/5cm long. With crochet hook, make 2 chs, 2"/5cm long. Attach 1 tassel to each end of ch. Fold ch in half and tack to lower edges at side seams.

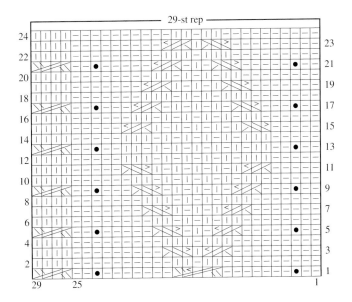

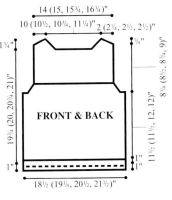

Stitch Key

- ☐ K on RS, p on WS
- ☐ P on RS, k on WS
- ● Make bobble
- 3-st BPC
- 3-st FPC
- 4-st BC
- 5-st cable

Set the stage for a little night magic. This sparkling, loose-fitting chemise features V-neck shaping and knit-in paillettes. Designer Kay Niederlitz reinterpreted this sleeveless evening dazzler for hand- or machine-knitters. Shown in size 36. The Paillette Dress first appeared in the Spring/Summer 1967 issue of the original Vogue Knitting magazine.

Paillette Dress

FOR INTERMEDIATE KNITTERS

SIZES
To fit 32 (34, 36, 38, 40)"/81 (86, 91, 96, 101)cm bust. Directions are for smallest size with larger sizes in parentheses. If there is only one figure, it applies to all sizes.

KNITTED MEASUREMENTS
● Bust at underarm 34 (36, 38, 40, 42)"/86 (91, 96, 101, 106)cm.
● Length 32½ (33¼, 34, 34¾, 35)"/82.5 (84.5, 86, 88, 89)cm.

MATERIALS
Original Yarn
● 4 (4, 4, 5, 5) 2oz/60g balls (each approx 300yds/275m) of Melrose/Stacy Charles *Cravenella* (wool/rayon 1) in sand platinum (grey)
Substitute Yarn
● 9 (9, 9, 11, 11) 1¾oz/50g balls (each approx 147yds/135m) of Filatura di Crosa/Tahki•Stacy Charles, Inc. *Sera* (wool/viscose/polyamide 1) in #2 grey
● One pair each sizes 2 and 4 (2.5 and 3mm) needles/standard gauge knitting machine OR SIZE TO OBTAIN GAUGE
● Small size steel crochet hook for finishing
● 6 (6, 7, 7, 7) bags of 1,000 matte grey ¾"/20mm paillettes

Note
The original yarn used for this dress is no longer available. A comparable substitution has been made, which is available at the time of printing. Check gauge of substitute yarns very carefully before beginning.

GAUGE
30 sts and 40 rows to 4"/10cm over paillette pat using size 4 (3mm) needles. FOR PERFECT FIT, TAKE TIME TO CHECK GAUGE.

HANDKNIT VERSION

STITCH GLOSSARY
Paillette Pat (multiple of 4 sts + 3)
Rows 1 and 3 (RS) Knit.
Row 2 Purl.
Row 4 *P3, place paillette in next st as foll: slide paillette close to needle and purl next st, then push paillette to front side of work—paillette st; rep from *, end p3.
Rows 5 and 7 Knit.
Row 6 Purl.
Row 8 *P1, work paillette st, p2; rep from *, end p1, work paillette st, p1.
Rep rows 1-8 for paillette pat.

Notes
1 Thread large number of paillettes on 2nd ball of yarn to work rows 4 and 8.
2 When shaping, omit paillettes that fall close to edge.
3 Make length changes before first dec row of pat.

BACK
With smaller needles, cast on 151 (159, 167, 175, 183) sts. Work in St st for 7 rows. K next row on WS (turning ridge). Change to larger needles. Work in paillette pat for 14 rows above turning ridge. Cont in pat, dec 1 st each side on next RS row, then every 16th row 6 (6, 6, 6, 0) times, every 14th row 5 (5, 5, 5, 12) times—127 (135, 143, 151, 157) sts. Work even until piece measures 19"/48cm from turning ridge. Mark waistline. Cont in paillette pat until piece measures 26 (26¼, 26½, 26¾, 27)"/66 (66.5, 67.5, 68, 68.5)cm above turning ridge.

Armhole shaping
Bind off 7 sts at beg of next 2 rows, then dec 1 st each side every 4th row 10 (10, 10, 11, 11) times—93 (101, 109, 115, 121) sts. Work even until armhole measures 5 (5½, 6, 6½, 6½)"/12.5 (14, 15.5, 16.5, 16.5)cm, end with a WS row.

Neck and shoulder shaping
Next row (RS) Work 24 (26, 28, 30, 32) sts, join 2nd ball of yarn and bind off 45 (49, 53, 55, 57) sts, work to end. Working both sides at once, dec 1 st at each neck edge every other row 4 times, AT SAME TIME, when armhole measures 6 (6½, 7, 7½, 7½)"/15.5 (16.5, 18, 19, 19)cm, bind off 10 (11, 12, 13, 14) sts from each shoulder edge twice.

FRONT
Work as for back until piece measures

same length as back to armhole, marking center st on last WS row.

Neck, armhole, shoulder shaping

Work armhole shaping as for back, AT SAME TIME, work V-neck shaping on next row as foll: Work to center st, join 2nd ball of yarn, k2tog (center st and next st), work to end. Working both sides at once, dec 1 st at each neck edge every 4th row 2 (3, 4, 4, 4) times, every other row 24 (25, 26, 27, 28) times. When same length as back to shoulder, shape shoulder as for back.

FINISHING

Do not press pieces. Sew shoulder seams. Sew side seams. Work 1 rnd of sc evenly around armholes and V-neck. Fold hem at turning ridge to WS and sew in place. Sew on additional paillettes if necessary to fill in.

MACHINE-KNIT VERSION

GAUGE

7.69 sts and 10 rows to 1"/2.5cm over jersey and paillette pat at Tension 7 on standard gauge (4.5mm) machine. FOR PERFECT FIT, TAKE TIME TO CHECK GAUGE.

Note

Use handknit version of paillette pat for reference.

Machine paillette pat set-up

Rows 1-4 Knit.
Paillette row 1 Pull out every 4th needle beg at either edge of needle bed. With 1-prong tool or tappet needle remove st from needle onto tool. Hang paillette on empty needle behind fabric and replace st back onto needle. Lift paillette over hook of needle—paillette is hanging on previously knit row. Cont hanging paillettes across row.
Rows 5-8 Knit.
Paillette row 2 Pull out 2nd needle from edge, and then every 4th needle across row and hang paillettes as above. Work rows 1-8 for pat. When shaping, keep to pat as established, omitting paillettes on end needles.

BACK

Set tension dial to tension 7. With waste yarn, cast on 155 (163, 171, 179, 187) sts, with extra st to right of 0. K 6 rows. Set RC to 0-0-0 with carriage on right. Change to main yarn. K 7 rows. Change tension to 4. K 1 row. Change to tension 7 and reset RC to 0-0-0.

Beg paillette pat: Work rows 1-7 of paillette pat.

Hem

*Pick up first st above waste yarn (main yarn) and hang on needle; rep from * to end. Cont working in paillette pat, AT SAME TIME at RC 15, dec 1 st each side every 15 rows 12 (12, 12, 0, 0) times, then every 14 rows 0 (0, 0, 13, 13) times—131 (139, 147, 153, 161) sts. At RC 190, mark each edge st for waistband. Cont to knit even until RC 260 (262, 264, 268, 270).

Armhole shaping

Bind off 7 sts at beg of next 2 rows, then dec 1 st each side every 4th row 9 (10, 10, 11, 11) times—99 (105, 113, 117, 125) sts. Knit until RC 310 (318, 324, 332, 336) to beg neck shaping with carriage at right.

Neck and shoulder shaping

Set carriage to hold. Put all but right 28 (29, 31, 32, 35) sts into holding position. At neck edge, hold 1 st every other row 5 times, AT SAME TIME when RC is at 319 (327, 333, 341, 343) shape shoulders over next 4 rows as foll: *Size 32:* hold 12 sts once, 11 sts once; *Size 34:* hold 12 sts twice; *Size 36:* hold 13 sts twice; *Size 38:* hold 14 sts once, 13 sts once; *Size 40:* hold 15 sts twice. K

shoulder sts off on waste yarn. With carriage at left reset to RC 310 (318, 324, 332, 336), hold 22 (24, 26, 27, 28) N's once and rep shaping as for right side. Return center 53 (57, 61, 63, 65) N's to working position and k 1 row with main yarn. K center N's off on waste yarn.

FRONT

Work as for back to armhole shaping—RC 260 (262, 264, 268, 270).

Neck, armhole, shoulder shaping

Work armhole shaping as for back, AT SAME TIME, work V-neck shaping as foll: With carriage on right set to hold, hold all N's to the left of 0. Keeping in pat as established, use 2-prong tool to dec 1 st at center every 4th row 2 (3, 4, 4, 4) times, then 1 st every 2 rows 25 (26, 27, 28, 29) times. At RC 319 (327, 333, 341, 343) shape shoulders as for back. Work left side of piece to correspond to right side as foll: With carriage on left, reset RC to 260 (262, 264, 268, 270). Work armhole shaping as for back and work first neck dec at RC 264 (266, 268, 272, 274). Cont to dec 1 st at neck edge every 4th row 0 (1, 2, 2, 2) times, every 2 rows 25 (26, 27, 28, 29) times. Work left shoulder to correspond to right shoulder.

FINISHING

With crochet hook, sl st shoulder seams tog. Remove waste yarn. Sew side seams. Sl st back neck sts. Remove waste yarn. Work sc edge as for handknit version.

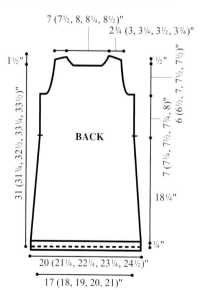

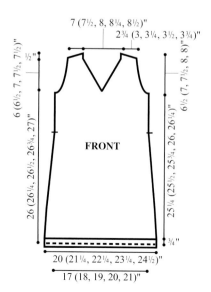

Striped Midriff Top

These sunny, breezy cropped tops capture the casual air of summer. They can be knit with red or navy and white stripes with a round or V-neck. Shown in size 36. The Striped Midriff Top first appeared in the Spring/Summer 1952 issue of the original *Vogue Knitting* magazine.

Photo: Fred Baker

Striped Midriff Top

VERY EASY VERY VOGUE

SIZES
To fit 32 (34, 36, 38)"/81 (86, 91, 96) cm bust. Directions are for smallest size with larger sizes in parentheses. If there is only one set of figures, it applies to all sizes.

KNITTED MEASUREMENTS
FOR BOTH STYLES:
● Bust 33 (35, 37, 39)"/83 (87, 93, 97)cm.
● Length 15 (16, 16½, 17½)"/38 (40, 41.5, 44)cm.

MATERIALS
Original Yarn
FOR V-NECK:
● 3 (3, 3, 4) 1¾oz/50g balls (each approx 230yds/210m) of Pingouin *Corrida No. 3* (cotton/acrylic 2) in #301 white (A)
● 3 (3, 3, 4) balls in #314 red (B)
FOR ROUND NECK:
● 3 (3, 3, 4) balls in #301 white (A)
● 3 (3, 3, 4) balls in #318 navy (B)
Substitute Yarn
FOR V-NECK:
● 4 (4, 4, 5) 1¾oz/50g balls (each approx 195yds/180m) of Grignasco/JCA *Marina* (cotton 2) in #001 white (A)
● 4 (4, 4, 5) in #673 red (B)

FOR ROUND NECK:
● 4 (4, 4, 5) balls in #001 white (A)
● 4 (4, 4, 5) balls in #717 dk blue (B)
● One pair of size 3 (3mm) needles
OR SIZE TO OBTAIN GAUGE

Note
The original yarn used for this sweater is no longer available. A comparable substitution has been made, which is available at the time of printing. Check gauge of substitute yarns very carefully before beginning.

GAUGE
28 sts and 40 rows to 4"/10cm over St st using size 3 (3mm) needles.
FOR PERFECT FIT, TAKE TIME TO CHECK GAUGE.

Note
If longer top is desired, work more rows in stripe pat before armhole shaping and be sure to buy extra yarn accordingly.

STITCH GLOSSARY
Stripe Pats
For V-neck: Work in St st (k on RS, p on WS) as foll: *8 rows B, 8 rows A; rep from * (16 rows) for stripe pat.
For round neck: Work in St st (k on RS, p on WS) as foll: *24 rows B, 24 rows A; rep from * (48 rows) for stripe pat.

BACK
With A, cast on 116 (122, 130, 136) sts. Work in St st for 10 rows for facing. P next 2 rows for turning ridge. Work in St st for 2 rows more. Work in desired stripe pat until piece measures 7½ (8, 8½, 9)"/19 (20, 21.5, 23)cm from turning ridge, or desired length to underarm.

Armhole shaping
Cont in stripe pat, bind off 7 (7, 8, 8) sts at beg of next 2 rows, 2 sts at beg of next 2 (2, 4, 4) rows. Dec 1 st each side every other row 5 times—88 (94, 96, 102) sts. Work even until armhole measures 4 (4½, 4½, 5)"/10 (11, 11, 12)cm, end with a WS row.

Neck shaping
For V-neck: Next row (RS) K43 (46, 47, 50) sts, join 2nd ball of yarn and bind off center 2 sts, work to end. Working both sides at once, bind off from each neck edge 2 sts 14 (15, 15, 16) times—15 (16, 17, 18) sts each side.
For round neck: Next row (RS) K36 (38, 39, 41) sts, join 2nd ball of yarn and bind off center 16 (18, 18, 20) sts, work to end. Working both sides at once, bind off from each neck edge 3 sts twice, 2 sts 2 (3, 3, 4) times, dec 1 st every other row 11 (10, 10, 9) times—15 (16, 17, 18) sts each side.
For both styles: Work even until arm-

hole measures 7½ (8, 8, 8½)"/19 (20, 20, 21)cm. Bind off sts each side for shoulders.

FRONT
Work as for back until armhole measures 3 (3½, 3½, 4)"/7.5 (8.5, 8.5, 9.5)cm.

Neck shaping
For V-neck: Next row (RS) K43 (46, 47, 50) sts, join 2nd ball of yarn and bind off center 2 sts, word to end. Working both sides at once, bind off from each neck edge 2 sts 8 (10, 10, 12) times, then dec 1 st every other row 12 (10, 10, 8) times—15 (16, 17, 18) sts each side.

For round neck: Next row (RS) K7 (39, 40, 42) sts, join 2nd ball of yarn and bind off center 14 (16, 16, 18) sts, work to end. Working both sides at once,

bind off from each neck edge 3 sts 0 (0, 0, 1) time, 2 sts 2 (3, 3, 2) times, dec 1 st every other row 18 (17, 17, 17) times—15 (16, 17, 18) sts each side.
For both styles: Work even until armhole measures 7½ (8, 8, 8½)"/19 (20, 20, 21)cm. Bind off sts each side for shoulders.

FINISHING
Block pieces to measurements.

Neckbands
For V-neck: Sew shoulder seams. With RS facing and B, beg at center front point, pick up and k 46 sts along right half of front neck and 40 sts along right half of back neck—86 sts. P 1 row. K 1 row. Bind off. Work other side to correspond. Fold bands to WS. Sew in place.
For round neck: Sew left shoulder

seam. With RS facing and B, beg at right shoulder, pick up and k 64 (66, 66, 68) sts along back neck, 74 (76, 76, 78) sts along front neck—138 (142, 142, 146) sts. P 1 row. K 1 row. Bind off. Sew right shoulder seam, including band. Fold band to WS. Sew in place.

Armhole bands
For both styles: With RS facing and B, pick up and k 45 (49, 49, 53) sts along one armhole edge to shoulder, pick up same number of sts along other edge—90 (98, 98, 106) sts. Work same as round neckband. Sew side seams. Fold lower edge of front and back to WS at turning ridge and sew in place.

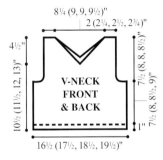

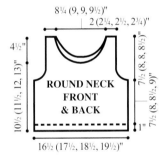

23.

This boldly-patterned pullover with foldback funnelneck is knit in super-soft mohair. Brightly colored spots put a playful spin on this mod classic. Shown in size Medium. The Polka-Dot Pullover first appeared in the Spring/Summer 1965 issue of the original *Vogue Knitting* magazine.

Polka-Dot Pullover

FOR INTERMEDIATE KNITTERS

SIZES
To fit Small (Medium and Large). Directions are for smallest size with larger sizes in parentheses. If there is only one figure, it applies to all sizes.

KNITTED MEASUREMENTS
● Bust 36 (41, 46)"/91.5 (104, 117)cm.
● Length 25½ (26, 26½)"/65 (66, 67.5)cm.
● Upper arm 14 (15, 16)"/41 (43, 46)cm.

MATERIALS
● 11 (12, 13) 1½oz/42g balls (each approx 90yds/82m) of Classic Elite Yarns *La Gran Mohair* (mohair/wool/nylon 4) in #6572 lime (MC)
● 1 ball each in the following contrasting colors: #6585 orange, #6593 blue, #6527 red, #6541 cranberry, and #6565 pink
● One pair each sizes 8 and 9 (5 and 5.5mm) needles OR SIZE TO OBTAIN GAUGE
● Stitch markers and holders

GAUGE
16 sts and 22 rows to 4"/10cm over St st using size 9 (5.5mm) needles.
FOR PERFECT FIT, TAKE TIME TO CHECK GAUGE.

Notes
1 Use a separate bobbin of contrasting yarn for each dot. When changing colors, twist yarns on WS to prevent holes in work.
2 Use colors as desired for dots. See photo for inspiration.

BACK
With smaller needles and MC, cast on 72 (82, 92) sts. Beg with a p row, work St st for 5 rows. P next row on RS for turning ridge. Change to larger needles and work in St st for 3 (5, 7) rows.

Beg chart pat
Row 1 (RS) Work 4 (9, 5) sts MC, work 18-st rep of chart 3 (3, 4) times, work first 10 sts once more, work 4 (9, 5) sts MC. Cont in pat as established until piece measures 16½"/42cm above turning ridge.

Armhole shaping
Bind off 4 (5, 5) sts at beg of next 2 rows. Dec 1 st each side every other

row 3 (3, 5) times—58 (66, 72) sts. Work even until armhole measures 8 (8½, 9)"/20.5 (21.5, 23)cm.

Shoulder shaping
Bind off 4 (5, 6) sts at beg of next 4 rows, 4 (6, 7) sts at beg of next 2 rows—34 sts. P next row on WS for turning ridge. Change to smaller needles and MC, work in St st for 5 rows, inc 1 st each side *every* row. Bind off.

FRONT
Work as for back.

SLEEVES
With smaller needles and MC, cast on 36 sts. Beg with a p row, work St st for 5 rows. P next row on RS for turning ridge. Change to larger needles and work in St st for 5 rows.

Beg chart pat
Row 1 (RS) Work 4 sts MC, work 18-st rep of chart once, work first 10 sts once more, work 4 sts MC. Cont in pat as established, AT SAME TIME, inc 1 st each side every 20th (12th, 10th row 4 (2, 8) times, every 0 (14th, 0) row 0 (4, 0) times—44 (48, 52) sts. Work even until piece measures 16½ (16½, 17)"/42 (42, 43)cm above turning ridge.

Cap shaping

Bind off 4 (5, 5) sts at beg of next 2 rows. Dec 1 st each side every other row 11 (12, 14) times. Bind off 2 sts at beg of next 4 rows. Bind off rem 6 sts.

FINISHING

Block pieces to measurements. Sew shoulder seams. Set in sleeves. Sew side and sleeve seams. Fold hems at lower edge of body, sleeves and at top of neck to WS at turning ridge and sew in place.

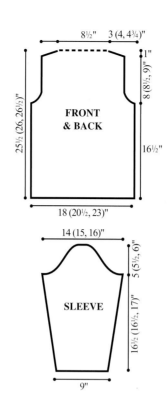

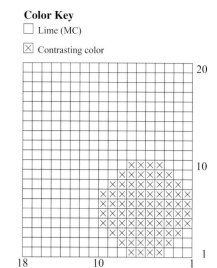

Color Key

☐ Lime (MC)

☒ Contrasting color

Argyle Short-Sleeved Top

This short-sleeved classic delivers a sporty sophistication that feels as right now as it did years ago. The cool-colored top features cap sleeves, a back neck opening, and crocheted edgings. Shown in size Medium. The Argyle Short-Sleeved Top first appeared in the Spring/Summer 1963 issue of the original *Vogue Knitting* magazine.

Argyle Short-Sleeved Top

FOR INTERMEDIATE KNITTERS

SIZES
To fit Small (Medium, Large). Directions are for smallest size with larger sizes in parentheses. If there is only one figure, it applies to all sizes.

KNITTED MEASUREMENTS
- Bust 34 (35, 39)"/86 (89, 99)cm.
- Waist 31 (33, 37)"/78.5 (83.5, 94)cm.
- Length 18¾ (19, 19½)"/47.5 (48, 49.5)cm.
- Upper arm 12 (12½, 13¼)"/30.5 (32, 33.5)cm.

MATERIALS
Original Yarn
- 4 (4, 5) 1¾oz/50g balls (each approx 124yds/115m) of GGH/Muench Yarns *Domino* (cotton/nylon 4) in #2 ivory (A)
- 2 (2, 3) balls in #9 lt green (B)
- 1 (1, 2) balls in #8 teal (C)

Substitute Yarn
- 5 (5, 6) 1¾oz/50g balls (each approx 110yds/101m) of Reynolds/JCA *Cantata* (cotton/nylon 4) in #101 ecru (A)
- 3 (3, 4) balls in #201 lt green
- 2 (2, 3) balls in #112 navy (C)
- One pair size 6 (4mm) needles OR SIZE TO OBTAIN GAUGE
- Bobbins
- Size E/4 (3.5mm) crochet hook

- One ½"/13mm button
- Tapestry needle

Note
The original yarn used for this sweater is no longer available. A comparable substitution has been made, which is available at the time of printing. Check gauge of substitute yarns very carefully before beginning.

GAUGE
20 sts and 26 rows to 4"/10cm in St st and chart pat using size 6 (4mm) needles. FOR PERFECT FIT, TAKE TIME TO CHECK GAUGE.

Note
Wind A and B onto bobbins and work each separate diamond and block of color with a separate bobbin. Work cross lines with C in duplicate st embroidery after pieces are knit.

BACK
With A, cast on 84 (88, 98) sts.

Beg chart
Row 1 (RS) K0 (2, 0) A, work 14-st rep of chart 6 (6, 7) times, k0 (2, 0) A. Working in St st, cont to foll chart in this way (working 24-row rep to end of piece) for 6 rows.
Next row (RS) Dec 1 st at beg and end of row. Rep this row every 6th row twice more—78 (82, 92) sts. Work even for 5 rows.

Next row (RS) Inc 1 st at beg and end of row. Rep this row every 8th row twice more—84 (88, 98) sts. Work even until 24-row rep has been worked 3 times and piece measures approx 11"/28cm from beg.

Armhole shaping
Bind off 4 (4, 5) sts at beg of next 2 rows. Dec 1 st each side every other row 4 (4, 6) times—68 (72, 76) sts. Work even through 4th rep of argyle. Armhole measures approx 3½"/9cm.

Back opening
Next row (RS) K34 (36, 38) sts, leave rem sts unworked. Working right half of back only, cont to work pat foll chart until armhole measures 6¾ (7, 7½)"/17 (17.5, 19)cm.

Shoulder shaping
Bind off 7 (7, 8) sts from shoulder edge (beg of RS rows) twice and 6 (8, 7) sts once. Bind off rem 14 (14, 15) sts for neck. Rejoin A and B and work left half of back to correspond, reversing shoulder shaping.

FRONT
Work as for back, omitting neck opening, until armhole measures 4½ (4¾, 5¼)"/11.5 (12, 13.5)cm.

Neck shaping
Next row (RS) Work 28 (30, 31) sts, join 2nd ball of yarn and bind off

center 12 (12, 14) sts, work to end. Working both sides at once, bind off 2 sts from each neck edge 3 times, dec 1 st twice. When same length as back to shoulders, shape shoulders as on back.

SLEEVES

With A, cast on 56 (56, 60) sts.

Beg chart

Row 1 (RS) K0 (0, 2) A, work 14-st rep of chart 4 times, k0 (0,2) A. Working in St st, cont to foll chart, inc 1 st each side every 6th row 2 (3, 3) times (working inc sts in A only). Work even on 60 (62, 66) sts until piece measures 4"/10cm from beg.

Cap shaping

Bind off 4 (4, 5) sts at beg of next 2 rows. Bind off 2 sts at beg of next 4 rows. Dec 1 st each side every other row 11 (12, 13) times. Bind off 3 sts at beg of next 4 rows. Bind off rem 10 sts.

FINISHING

Block pieces to measurements. With tapestry needle and C, work cross lines foll chart in duplicate st on all pieces. Sew shoulder seams. Set in sleeves. Sew side and sleeve seams. With crochet hook and A, work 2 rnds sc around neck, sleeve and lower edges for facings. Turn facings to WS and sew in place. Work 1 row sc around back neck opening with a ch-8 button loop at top. Sew on button at back neck.

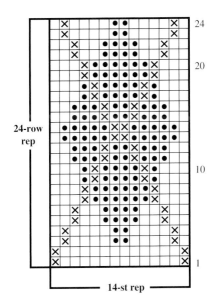

Color key

☐ Ecru (A)

● Lt. Green (B)

☒ Navy (C) in duplicate st

24-row rep

14-st rep

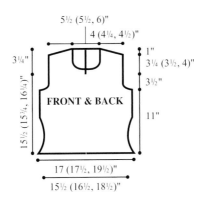

5½ (5½, 6)"

4 (4¼, 4½)"

3¼"

1"
3¼ (3½, 4)"

3½"

15½ (15¾, 16¼)"

FRONT & BACK

11"

17 (17½, 19½)"

15½ (16½, 18½)"

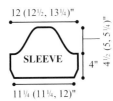

12 (12½, 13¼)"

4½ (5, 5¼)"

SLEEVE

4"

11¼ (11¼, 12)"

Elegant and understated, this fine-gauge cashmere turtleneck is as much a favorite with the sophisticated woman of today as it was back in 1951. Flattering lean lines and touchable texture give the street-smart classic unbeatable charm. Shown in size Small. The Cashmere Turtleneck first appeared in the Spring/Summer 1951 issue of the original Vogue Knitting magazine.

Cashmere Turtleneck

FOR INTERMEDIATE KNITTERS

SIZES**

To fit X-Small (Small, Medium, Large, X-Large, XX-Large). Directions are for smallest size with larger sizes in parentheses. If there is only one figure, it applies to all sizes.

**Due to the nature of the yarn and stitch, this garment will stretch to be wider than the knitted measurements when worn.

KNITTED MEASUREMENTS

● Bust 34 (38, 41, 44, 47½, 51)"/82.5 (96.5, 104, 111.5, 120.5, 129.5)cm.
● Length 24 (24½, 25, 26, 26½, 27)"/61 (62.5, 63.5, 66.5, 67.5, 69)cm.
● Upper arm 13 (14, 15, 16½, 17½, 18½)"/33 (35.5, 38, 42, 44.5, 47)cm.

MATERIALS

● 20 (23, 25, 28, 30, 33) .88oz/25g balls (each approx 107yds/98m) of Jaeger Handknits *Cashmere 4 Ply* (cashmere/polyamide 2) in #0122 blue
● One pair each sizes 2 and 3 (2.5 and 3mm) needles OR SIZE TO OBTAIN GAUGE
● Size 2 (2.5mm) circular needle, 16"/40cm long
● Cable needle (cn)

GAUGE

34 sts and 35 rows to 4"/10cm over chart pat (slightly stretched) using size 3 (3mm) needles. FOR PERFECT FIT, TAKE TIME TO CHECK GAUGE.

STITCH GLOSSARY

8-st RC

Sl 4 sts to cn and hold to *back*, k4, k4 from cn.

BACK

With smaller needles, cast on 146 (160, 174, 188, 202, 216) sts. Work in k2, p2 rib for 3"/7.5cm, end with a WS row. Change to larger needles.

Beg cable chart

Next row (RS) Work 14-st rep of chart 10 (11, 12, 13, 14, 15) times, work last 6 sts once more. Cont in pat as established until piece measures 16 (16, 16, 16½, 16½, 16½)"/40.5 (40.5, 40.5, 42, 42, 42)cm from beg.

Armhole shaping

Bind off 8 (8, 8, 9, 9, 9) sts at beg of next 2 rows, 3 sts at beg of next 0 (0, 0, 2, 4, 6) rows, 2 sts at beg of next 0 (4, 6, 2, 4, 4) rows. Dec 1 st each side on next row, then every other row 8 (7, 8, 9, 7, 6) times more—112 (120, 128, 140, 148, 158) sts. Work even until armhole measures 7½ (8, 8½, 9, 9½, 10)"/19 (20.5, 21.5, 23, 24, 25.5)cm.

Shoulder shaping

Bind off 12 (13, 14, 16, 17, 19) sts at beg of next 4 rows, 12 (14, 15, 17, 17, 18) sts at beg of next 2 rows. Bind off rem 40 (40, 42, 42, 46, 46) sts for back neck.

FRONT

Work as for back until armhole measures 5 (5½, 6, 6½, 7, 7½)"/13 (14.5, 15.5, 17, 18, 19.5)cm, end with a WS row.

Neck shaping

Next row (RS) Work 44 (48, 51, 57, 59, 64) sts, join 2nd ball of yarn and bind off center 24 (24, 26, 26, 30, 30) sts, work to end. Working both sides at once, dec 1 st at each neck edge every other row 8 times. Work even until same length as back to shoulder. Shape shoulder as for back.

SLEEVES

With smaller needles cast on 70 (70, 70, 74, 74, 74) sts. Work in k2, p2 rib for 3"/7.5cm, inc 6 (6, 6, 2, 2, 2) sts on last WS row—76 sts. Change to larger needles.

Beg cable chart

Next row (RS) Work 14-st rep of chart 5 times, work last 6 sts once more. Cont in pat as established, inc 1 st each side (working inc sts into pat) every 6th (4th, 4th, 2nd, 2nd, 2nd) row 13 (7, 16, 12, 11, 18) times, every 8th (6th, 6th, 4th, 4th, 4th) row 5 (15, 10, 20, 25, 23)

times—112 (120, 128, 140, 148, 158) sts. Work even until piece measures 17½ (17½, 18, 18, 18, 18½)"/44.5 (44.5, 45.5, 45.5, 45.5, 47)cm from beg.

Cap shaping

Bind off 8 (8, 9, 9, 9, 9) sts at beg of next 2 rows, 3 sts at beg of next 0 (0, 0, 0, 2, 4) rows, 2 sts at beg of next 0 (0, 2, 4, 4, 4) rows. Dec 1 st each side on next row, then every other row 19 (21, 22, 24, 25, 26) times more. Bind off 5 sts at beg of next 4 rows, 6 sts at beg of next 2 rows. Bind off rem 24 (28, 28, 32, 32, 34) sts.

FINISHING

Block pieces to measurements. Sew shoulder seams.

Neckband

With RS facing and circular needle, pick up and k 128 (128, 132, 132, 140, 140) sts evenly around neck edge. Join and work in k2, p2 rib for 5"/12.5cm. Bind off in rib. Set in sleeves. Sew side and sleeve seams.

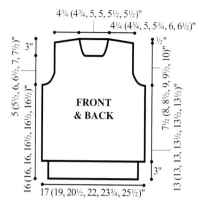

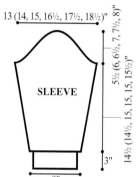

VOGUE KNITTING **38** VINTAGE COLLECTION

Stitch Key

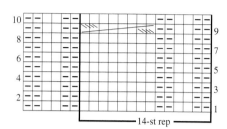

☐ K on RS, p on WS

⊟ P on RS, k on WS

▨ 8-st RC

Crocheted Flower Pullover

Applied crocheted flowers and leaves sprouting from a flowerpot patch pocket add a cheery finish to this casual stockinette-stitch pullover. It's standard-fitting with set-in sleeves, boatneck, and hemmed edges. Shown in size 34. The Crocheted Flower Pullover first appeared in the Spring/Summer 1960 issue of the original Vogue Knitting magazine.

Crocheted Flower Pullover

FOR INTERMEDIATE KNITTERS

SIZES
To fit 32 (34, 36, 38, 40)"/81 (86, 91, 96, 101)cm bust. Directions are for smallest size with larger sizes in parentheses. If there is only one figure, it applies to all sizes.

KNITTED MEASUREMENTS
● Bust 37 (39, 41, 43, 45)"/94 (99, 104, 109, 114)cm.
● Length 20 (20¼, 20½, 21, 21½)"/51 (51.5, 52, 53.5, 54.5)cm.
● Upper arm 12¼ (13, 13¾, 14½, 15)"/31 (33, 35, 37, 38)cm.

MATERIALS
Original Yarn
● 9 (10, 10, 11, 12) 1¾oz/50g balls (each approx 112yds/102m) of Anny Blatt *Coton d'Egypt No. 2* (cotton 3) in #530 ecru (MC)
● 1 ball each #408 lt blue (A), #602 coral (B) and #342 navy (C)
Substitute Yarn
● 10 (11, 11, 12, 13) 1¾oz/50g balls (each approx 108yds/99m) of Garnstudio/Aurora Yarns *Muskat* (cotton 2) #08 ecru (MC)
● 1 ball each #02 lt blue (A); #08 coral (B); #13 navy (C)
● One pair each size 2 and 3 (2.5 and 3mm) needles OR SIZE TO OBTAIN GAUGE
● Size D/3 (3mm) crochet hook

Note
The original yarn used for this sweater is no longer available. A comparable substitution has been made, which is available at the time of printing. Check gauge of substitute yarns very carefully before beginning.

GAUGE
24 sts and 32 rows to 4"/10cm over St st using size 3 (3mm) needles.
FOR PERFECT FIT, TAKE TIME TO CHECK GAUGE.

BACK
With smaller needles and MC, cast on 111 (117, 123, 129, 135) sts. Work 7 rows in St st .
Next row (WS) Knit (turning ridge for hem). Change to larger needles. Cont to work in St st for 7 rows.
Next row (WS) Knit (hemline). Cont to work in St st until piece measures 12"/30.5cm above turning ridge.

Armhole shaping
Bind off 7 (7, 8, 8, 8) sts at beg of next 2 rows. Dec 1 st each side every other row 8 (8, 8, 8, 9) times—81 (87, 91, 97, 101) sts. Work even until armhole measures 5 (6, 6¼, 6¾, 7¼)"/14.5 (15, 16, 17, 18.5)cm, end with a RS row.
Next row (WS) Knit. Work even in St st until armhole measures 7 (7¼, 7½, 8, 8½)"/18 (18.5, 19, 20.5, 21.5)cm.

Shoulder and neck shaping
Bind off 4 (4, 5, 5, 5) sts at beg of next 4 (8, 2, 6, 8) rows, then 3 (0, 4, 4, 0) sts at beg of next 4 (0, 6, 2, 0) rows—53 (55, 57, 59, 61) sts. Change to smaller needles and k 1 row on WS for turning ridge.

Neck facing
Cast on 3 (0, 4, 4, 0) sts at beg of next 4 (0, 6, 2, 0) rows, 4 (4, 5, 5, 5) sts at beg of next 4 (8, 2, 6, 8) rows—81 (87, 91, 97, 101) sts. Work even for 10 rows. Bind off.

FRONT
Work as for back.

SLEEVES
With smaller needles and MC, cast on 58 (60, 64, 66, 70) sts. Work 7 rows in St st.
Next row (WS) Knit (turning ridge for hem). Change to larger needles and work in St st for 7 rows.
Next row (WS) Knit. Cont in St st, AT SAME TIME, when piece measures 1"/2.5cm above turning ridge, inc 1 st each side every 8th row 0 (0, 0, 2, 2) times, every 10th row 0 (6, 6, 8, 8) times, then every 12th row 8 (3, 3, 0, 0) times—74 (78, 82, 86, 90) sts. Work even until piece measures 13"/33cm above turning ridge.

Cap shaping
Bind off 7 (7, 8, 8, 8) sts at beg of next

2 rows. Dec 1 st each side every other row 14 (15, 16, 18, 20) times. Bind off 2 sts at beg of next 6 rows. Bind off rem 20 (22, 22, 22, 22) sts.

POCKET

With larger needles and C, cast on 27 sts. Work in St st for 3½"/9cm, end with a RS row. K 1 row on WS. Cont in St st until pocket measures 4½"/11.5cm from beg, end with a RS row. Change to smaller needles. K 1 row (turning ridge). Work 7 rows in St st. Bind off. Fold at turning ridge and sew hem to WS.

FINISHING

Block pieces to measurements. Sew shoulder seams. Set in sleeves. Sew side and sleeve seams. Turn hem facing to WS and sew in place. Tack ends of neck facings to armhole seams. Sew pocket to front 2¾"/7cm in from left side seam and 1"/2.5cm above purl ridge at top of hem.

Stems and leaves

(**Note:** Leave a 12"/30.5cm end of yarn for sewing when beg each piece and when fastening off.) With crochet hook and A, ch 29 for stem and vein of leaf. **Large leaf:** 1 sc in 2nd ch from hook, * 1 sc in next ch, 1 dc in each of next 2 ch, 1 tr in each of next 2 ch, 1 dtr in each of next 4 ch, 1 tr in each of next 2 ch, 1 dc in each of next 2 ch, 1 sc in each of next 2 ch*; pass yarn under stem and ch 1 in front of stem—bottom of leaf—sc in same ch as last sc on opposite side of leaf; rep between *'s, sl st in ch at end of leaf. Fasten off. Insert hook under ch 1 at bottom of leaf and join yarn with sl st, ch 29. **2nd Large leaf:** Work as for first large leaf. Fasten off. Ch 10 for stem of lower flower, sl st under ch at bottom of 2nd leaf. Ch 29. **Small leaf:** Work as for large leaf omitting the 4 dtr's. Fasten off. Join yarn with sl st under ch 1 at bottom of small leaf, ch 23. **2nd Small leaf:** Work as for first small leaf. Fasten off. Join yarn with sl st

under ch at bottom of 2nd small leaf, ch 10 for stem of top flower.

Flowers (make 2)

With B, ch 5. Join with sl st to form a ring. Ch 1, 2 sc in each of 5 chs—10 sc. **Back petals:** *Sl st in back lp of next st, ch 6, 3 dtr in back lp of next st, ch 5; rep from * 4 times more, sl st in same st as beg st. Ch 1. **Front petals:** *Sl st in front lp of next st, ch 5, 2 tr in front lp of next st, ch 4; rep from * 4 times more; sl st in same st as beg st. Fasten off, draw yarn through to WS. Sew leaves and stems on front with lower end of stem ½"/1.5cm inside pocket opening and top end of stem approx 2½"/6.5cm below purl ridge at neck. Sew on flowers with centers at end of stems.

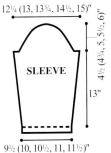

LAZY DAISY STITCH

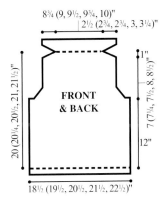

8¾ (9, 9½, 9¾, 10)"
2½ (2¾, 2¾, 3, 3¼)"

FRONT & BACK

20 (20¼, 20½, 21, 21½)"
1"
7 (7¼, 7½, 8, 8½)"
12"

18½ (19½, 20½, 21½, 22½)"

12¼ (13, 13¾, 14½, 15)"

SLEEVE

4½ (4¾, 5, 5½, 6)"
13"

9½ (10, 10½, 11, 11½)"

Women's Fall/Winter

Winter wools in stunning stitch patterns are welcome antidotes to the cold weather months. Here is a selection of wonderful designs suitable for outdoor sport, office attire, or casual dressing.

This Nordic knit cardigan looks good on or off the slopes. It has a relaxed fit and stylish zip-front, with mitered colorwork border panels knit from side to side. Shown in size Medium. The Nordic-Style Ski Sweater first appeared in the Fall/Winter 1963 issue of the original *Vogue Knitting* magazine.

Nordic-Style Ski Sweater

Photo: Francesco Scavullo

FOR INTERMEDIATE KNITTERS

SIZES
To fit Small (Medium, Large). Directions are for smallest size with larger sizes in parentheses. If there is only one figure, it applies to all sizes.

KNITTED MEASUREMENTS
● Bust (closed) 42½ (45, 48)"/108 (114.5, 122)cm.
● Length 24½ (25, 26)"/62 (63.5, 66)cm.
● Upper arm 15 (15½, 16½)"/38 (39.5, 42)cm.

MATERIALS
Original Yarn
● 8 (9, 10) 1¾oz/50g skeins (each approx 132yds/120m) of GGH for Meunch Yarns *Fun-uni* (wool/nylon 6) in #17 light green (MC)
● 2 (3, 3) skeins in #10 dk green (A)
● 1 (2, 2) skeins in #6 red (B)
Substitute Yarn
● 12 (14, 15) 1¾oz/50g skeins (each approx 90yds/83m) of Berroco, Inc. *Plush* (acrylic 5) in #1904 green (MC)
● 3 (5, 5) balls in 1911 teal (A)
● 2 (3, 3) balls #1908 red (B)
● One pair each sizes 5 and 11 (3.75 and 8mm) needles OR SIZE TO OBTAIN GAUGE
● One separating zipper, 24"/60cm long

● Crochet hook size J/10 (6mm)
● Stitch markers

Note
The original yarn used for this sweater is no longer available. A comparable substitution has been made, which is available at the time of printing. Check gauge of substitute yarns very carefully before beginning.

GAUGE
11 sts and 14 rows to 4"/10cm over St st using size 11 (8mm) needles with 2 strands held tog. FOR PERFECT FIT, TAKE TIME TO CHECK GAUGE.

Note
Cardigan is worked with 2 strands of yarn held together throughout, unless specified otherwise.

BACK
With larger needles and single strand of A, cast on 45 (49, 53) sts. K 1 row, p 1 row. Place marker at each end of row to mark hem. With 2 strands of yarn held tog, work 16 rows of Back border chart. Cont with MC until piece measures 15 (15, 15½)"/38 (38, 39.5)cm above hem markers, end with a WS row.

Armhole shaping
Bind off 2 sts at beg of next 2 rows. Dec 1 st each side on next row, then every other row twice more—35 (39,

43) sts. Work even until armhole measures 8½ (9, 9½)"/21.5 (23, 24)cm, end with a WS row.

Shoulder shaping
Bind off 5 (6, 6) sts at beg of next 2 rows, 6 (7, 7) sts at beg of next 2 rows. Bind off rem 13 (13, 17) sts.

LEFT FRONT
With larger needles and single strand of A, cast on 30 (32, 34) sts. K 1 row, p 1 row. Place marker at each end of row to mark hem. With 2 strands of yarn held tog, work 16 rows of Lower left front border chart, dec 1 st at end of row on 3rd row, then every other row 6 times more—23 (25, 27) sts. Cont with MC until piece measures same length as back to underarm, end with a WS row.

Armhole shaping
Next row (RS) Bind off 5 (5, 6) sts, work to end. Dec 1 st at armhole edge every row 7 (7, 8) times—11 (13, 13) sts. Work even until same length as back to shoulder shaping. Shape shoulder at beg of RS rows as for back.

RIGHT FRONT
Work to correspond to left front, reversing shaping and working 16 rows of Lower right front border chart.

LEFT FRONT EDGE BORDER
With larger needles and single strand of

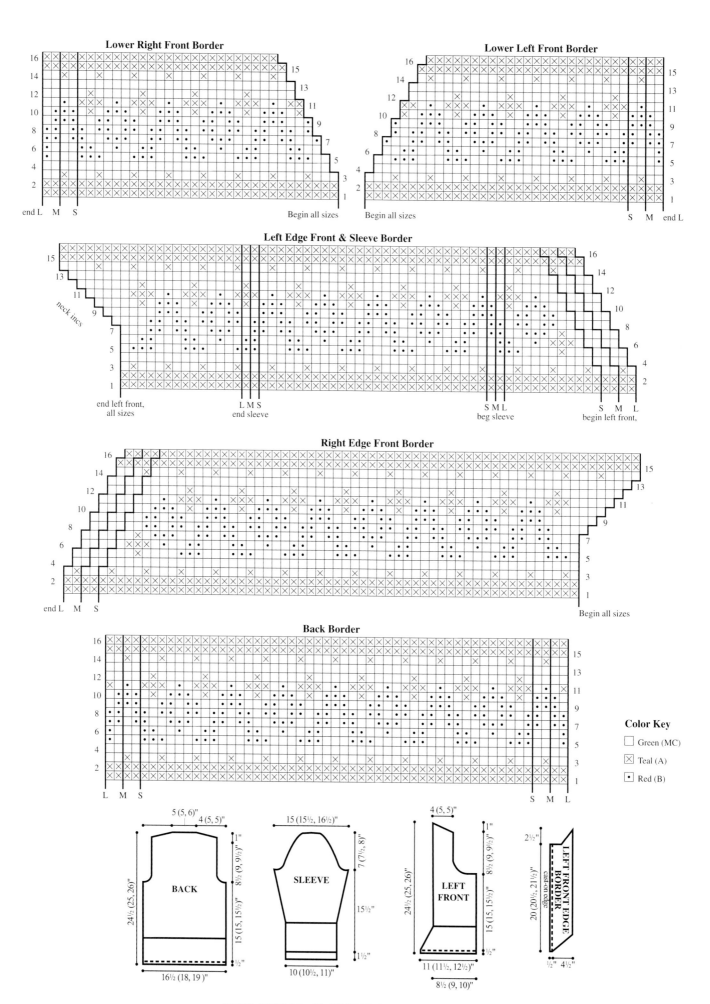

Lower Right Front Border

Lower Left Front Border

Left Edge Front & Sleeve Border

Right Edge Front Border

Back Border

Color Key
☐ Green (MC)
☒ Teal (A)
• Red (B)

A, cast on 55 (57, 59) sts. K 1 row, p 1 row. Place marker at each end of row to mark hem. With 2 strands of yarn held tog, work 16 rows of Left front edge border chart, dec 1 st at beg of row on 3rd row, then every other row 6 times more, AT SAME TIME, inc 1 st at LH side on 7th row, then every row 6 times more—55 (57, 59) sts. Bind off all sts.

RIGHT FRONT EDGE BORDER
Work to correspond to Left front edge border, reversing shaping and working 16 rows of Right front edge border chart.

SLEEVES
With smaller needles and 2 strands of MC, cast on 21 (23, 25) sts. Work in k1, p1 rib for 1½"/4cm, inc 6 sts evenly across last (WS) row—27 (29, 31) sts. Change to larger needles. Work 16 rows of Sleeve border chart, then cont with MC, inc 1 st each side on next row, then every 4th row 3 times, every 6th row 3 times—41 (43, 45) sts. Work even until piece measures 17"/43cm from beg, end with a WS row.

Cap shaping
Bind off 2 sts at beg of next 2 rows. Dec 1 st each side every row 5 times, every other row 5 (6, 7) times, then every row 6 times. Bind off rem 5 sts.

FINISHING
Block pieces. Sew shoulder seams. Sew bound-off edge of Left front edge border along left front edge. Sew Right front edge border to right front in same way. Turn hem of each front edge border to WS at markers and sew in place.

Neckband
With RS facing, larger needles and 2 strands of A, beg at right front edge and pick up and k 45 (45, 49) sts evenly around neck edge. P 1 row on WS. Change to single strand of A and work 2 rows in St st. Bind off. Fold band to WS and sew in place. Sew side and sleeve seams. Set in sleeves. Sew mitered seam at corner of each front. With crochet hook and 2 strands A, work 1 row of sl st along each mitered seam. Turn hem at lower edge to WS at markers and sew in place. Sew in zipper.

Photo: Tom Palumbo

Chic and sophisticated or bold and bright—the look of this machine-knit turtleneck dramatically changes depending on the yarn colors chosen. Shown in size Small. The Tri-Colored Raglan Pullover first appeared in the Fall/Winter 1968 issue of the original *Vogue Knitting* magazine.

Tri-Colored Raglan Pullover

VERY EASY VERY VOGUE

SIZES
To fit Small (Medium, Large and X-Large). Directions are for smallest size with larger sizes in parentheses. If there is only one figure, it applies to all sizes.

KNITTED MEASUREMENTS
● Bust at underarm 36 (38, 40, 42)"/91.5 (96.5, 101.5, 106.5)cm.
● Length 23 (23½, 25, 25½)"/58.5 (59.5, 63.5, 65)cm.
● Upper arm 12½ (13, 13½, 14½)"/32 (33, 34, 37)cm.

MATERIALS
Original Yarn
● 5 (5, 6, 6) 1¾oz/50g balls (each approx 93yds/85m) of Pinguoin *Borneo* (viscose/polyamide) in #3307 Saphir (A)
● 4 (4, 5, 5) balls each of #3106 Turquoise (B) and #4108 Anis (C)
Substitute Yarn
● 4 (4, 5, 5) 1¾oz/50g balls (each approx 120yds/110m) of Filatura di Crosa/Tahki•Stacy Charles, Inc. *Brilla* (cotton/viscose 3) in #332 navy (A)
● 4 (4, 4, 4) balls each in #333 turquoise (B) and #326 light green (C)
● Studio SK-860 knitting machine or any mid-gauge 6.5mm machine*
● Size 1 (6mm) crochet hook
● 4 large buttons
● 4 snaps
*If desired, use standard-gauge machine and adjust tension accordingly.

Note
The original yarn used for this sweater is no longer available. A comparable substitution has been made, which is available at the time of printing. Check gauge of substitute yarns very carefully before beginning.

GAUGE
22 sts and 30 rows to 4"/10cm at Ten over jersey.
FOR PERFECT FIT, TAKE TIME TO CHECK GAUGE.

BACK
With A, cast on 100 (104, 110, 116) sts.
RC000. Knit even to RC 64 (64, 68, 68) for 8½ (8½, 9, 9)"/21.5 (21.5, 23, 23)cm. Break off A. With B, knit even to RC 112 (112, 120, 120) for 15 (15, 16, 16)"/38 (38, 40.5, 40.5)cm from beg.

Raglan shaping
RC 113 (113, 121, 121) and 114 (114, 122, 122). With B, bind off 4 sts at beg of next 2 rows. (**Note:** Work raglan decs one st in from edge.)
RC 115 (115, 123, 123). Dec 1 st each end of row.
RC 116 (116, 124, 124). Knit 3 rows even.
RC 119 (119, 127, 127)—122 (122, 130, 130). Rep last 4 rows once more. Break off B.
RC 123 (123, 131, 131)—172 (176, 188, 192). With C, cont to dec 1 st each end of every other row 25 (27, 29,

31) times more. Bind off rem 38 (38, 40, 42) sts.

FRONT
Work same as back to RC 112 (112, 120, 120).

Raglan shaping
RC 113 (113, 121, 121)—114 (114, 122, 122). With B, bind off 4 sts at beg of next 2 rows. (**Note:** Work raglan decs one st in from edge.)
RC 115 (115, 123, 123). Dec 1 st each end of row.
RC 116 (116, 124, 124)—118 (118, 126, 126). Knit 3 rows even.
RC 119 (119, 127, 127)—122 (122, 130, 130). Rep last 4 rows once more. Break off B.
RC 123 (123, 131, 131)—130 (130, 138, 138). With C, rep last 4 rows twice more.
RC 131 (131, 139, 139)—162 (166, 176, 180). Dec 1 st each end every other row 16 (18, 19, 20) times—52 (52, 56, 58) sts.

Neck shaping
Bind off center 26 (26, 26, 28) sts.
RC 162 (166, 176, 180)—172 (176, 188, 192). Working each side separately, cont raglan decs at arm edge every other row 5 (5, 6, 6) times. AT THE SAME TIME, at neck edge, dec 1 st every other row 5 (5, 6, 6) times. Bind off rem 3 sts. Work second side to correspond to first side, reversing shaping.

SLEEVES

With A, cast on 44 (46, 48, 50) sts.
RC000. Knit even to RC 64 (64, 68, 68) for 8½ (8½, 9, 9)"/21.5 (21.5, 23, 23)cm, then with B knit to RC 112 (112, 120, 120) for 6½ (6½, 7, 7)"/16.5 (16.5, 18, 18)cm; AT SAME TIME, inc 1 st each end every ¾"/2cm 12 (13, 14, 15) times—68 (72, 76, 80) sts.

Raglan cap

RC 113 (113, 121, 121)—114 (114, 122, 122). With B, bind off 4 sts at beg of next 2 rows. (**Note:** Work raglan decs one st in from edge.)
RC 115 (115, 123, 123). Dec 1 st each end of row.
RC 116 (116, 124, 124)—118 (118, 126, 126). Knit 3 rows even.
RC 119 (119, 127, 127)—122 (122, 130, 130). Rep last 4 rows once more. Break off B.
RC 123 (123, 131,131)—138 (146, 146). With C, rep last 4 rows 4 times more.
RC 139 (139, 147, 147)—172 (176, 188, 192). Dec 1 st each end every other row 17 (19, 21, 23) times. Bind off rem 14 sts.

FINISHING

Sew sleeve to right back and front armhole. Sew second sleeve to left back armhole and front armhole to top of B stripe. With right side facing and C, work 1 row sc along front edge of left raglan seam. Fasten off. With C, work 4 rows of sc along upper sleeve edge of raglan seam for underlap. Sew sleeve seams. With A, work 1 rnd sc around lower and sleeve edges.

Collar

With C, cast on 51 (54, 57, 60) sts plus 4 sts for underlap. Knit even to RC 46 for 6"/15cm. Bind off. Sew collar to neckline. With right side facing and C, work 1 row sc along side edges of collar. Roll collar to right side and tack. Close seam with snap fasteners. Sew on buttons.

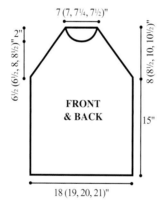

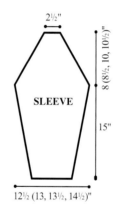

Fair Isle Cardigan

Fair-Isle bands, traditional cardigan styling—the best details endure the test of time. This color classic features set-in sleeves and a deep ribbed waistband. Shown in size Medium. The Fair Isle Cardigan first appeared in the Fall/Winter 1951 issue of the original *Vogue Knitting* magazine.

Photo: Fred Baker

Fair Isle Cardigan

FOR INTERMEDIATE KNITTERS

SIZES
To fit Small (Medium, Large, X-Large). Directions are for smallest size with larger sizes in parentheses. If there is only one figure, it applies to all sizes.

KNITTED MEASUREMENTS
● Bust (buttoned) 34¾ (36¾, 40¼, 42¾)"/88 (93, 102, 108.5)cm.
● Length 20½ (21¼, 21¾, 22¾)"/52.5 (54, 55, 57.5)cm.
● Upper arm 13 (13½, 14, 14½)"/32.5 (33.5, 35, 36)cm.

MATERIALS
● 8 (8, 9, 10) 1¾oz/50g balls (each approx 135yds/125m) of Patons® Country Garden DK (wool 3) in #73 grey (MC)
● 1 ball each in #35 aqua (A), #69 ruby (B), #43 olive (C), #29 blue (D), #45 peach (E), #25 cranberry (F) and #56 med green (G)
● One pair each sizes 3 and 5 (3 and 3.75mm) needles OR SIZE TO OBTAIN GAUGE
● Seven ⅝"/15mm buttons
● Stitch holders

GAUGE
24 sts and 30 rows to 4"/10cm over St st using size 5 (3.75mm) needles. FOR PERFECT FIT, TAKE TIME TO CHECK GAUGE.

Note
Fair Isle band is worked on fronts and sleeves only.

BACK
With smaller needles and MC, cast on 101 (107, 117, 125) sts. Work in k1, p1 rib for 3½"/9cm. Change to larger needles and work in St st until piece measures 12½ (13, 13, 13½)"/32 (33, 33, 34)cm from beg.

Armhole shaping
Bind off 6 (6, 6, 7) sts at beg of next 2 rows, 2 sts at beg of next 2 (2, 4, 4) rows, dec 1 st each side every other row 3 (5, 6, 6) times—79 (81, 85, 91) sts. Work even until armhole measures 7 (7¼, 7¾, 8¼)"/18 (18.5, 19.5, 21)cm.

Shoulder shaping
Bind off 5 sts at beg of next 6 (6, 8, 4) rows, 4 (4, 0, 6) sts at beg of next 2 (2, 0, 4) rows. Bind off rem 41 (43, 45, 47) sts for back neck.

LEFT FRONT
With smaller needles and MC, cast on 60 (63, 68, 72) sts. Work in k1, p1 rib for 3½"/9cm. Change to larger needles.
Next row (RS) K51 (54, 59, 63), place last 9 sts on a holder for front band. Cont in St st until piece measures same as back to armhole.

Armhole shaping
(**Note:** Fair Isle chart begins during the armhole shaping for some sizes.)
Bind off from armhole edge (beg of RS rows) same as for back, AT SAME TIME, when armhole measures ¾ (1, 1½, 2)"/2 (2.5, 4, 5)cm, work Fair Isle chart so that the last st at front edge is last st of chart. Cont to foll chart through row 27, then cont with MC on all 40 (41, 43, 46) sts for 10 more rows. Armhole measures approx 5¾ (6, 6½, 7)"/14.5 (15, 16.5, 18)cm.

Neck shaping
Next row (WS) Bind off 6 (6, 7, 7) sts, p to end. Cont to bind off from neck edge 5 (5, 5, 6) sts once, 4 sts once, 3 sts once, 2 sts once and 1 st 1 (2, 2, 2) times, AT SAME TIME, when same length as back to shoulder, shape shoulder at side edge as for back.

RIGHT FRONT
Work as for left front, reversing shaping and beg Fair Isle chart at front edge with last st of chart. Work 2 buttonholes on lower band, the first one at ½"/1.5cm from lower edge, the last one 2 rows below end of rib band as foll:
Buttonhole row (RS) Rib 4, k2tog, yo, work to end.

SLEEVES
With smaller needles and MC, cast on 45 sts. Work in k1, p1 rib for 3½"/9cm,

inc 15 sts evenly spaced across last WS row—60 sts. Change to larger needles and work in St st for 4 rows.

Beg Fair Isle chart

Next row (RS) Work 12-st rep of chart 5 times. Cont to foll chart through row 27, then cont with MC only, AT SAME TIME, inc 1 st each side every 8th (8th, 8th, 6th) row 9 (10, 12, 13) times—78 (80, 84, 86) sts. Work even until piece measures 17½"/44.5cm from beg.

Cap shaping

Bind off 5 sts at beg of next 2 rows, 2 sts at beg of next 2 rows. Dec 1 st each side every other row 15 (16, 18, 19) times. Bind off 2 sts at beg of next 6 rows. Bind off rem 22 sts.

FINISHING

Block pieces to measurements. With smaller needles, work across 9 left front band sts in k1, p1 rib until band fits to neck shaping. Sl sts to a holder. Place markers for 6 buttons along band, the first 2 markers in lower band opposite buttonhole, the last marker at 2½ (2¾, 3, 3)"/6.5 (7, 7.5, 7.5)cm down from neck shaping, and 3 others spaced evenly between. Work right front band to correspond, working 4 more buttonholes opposite markers. Sew shoulder seams. Sew band to front edges. Pick up and k 119 (123, 127, 131) sts evenly around neck edge, including sts from holders. Work in k1, p1 rib for 1"/2.5cm, working 1 more buttonhole after ½"/1.25cm. Bind off in rib when band is completed. Sew sleeves into armholes. Sew side and sleeve seams. Sew on buttons.

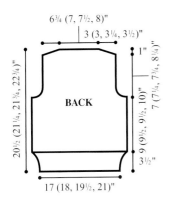

6¾ (7, 7½, 8)"
3 (3, 3¼, 3½)"
1"
BACK
20½ (21¼, 21¾, 22¾)"
7 (7¼, 7¾, 8¼)"
9 (9½, 9½, 10)"
3½"
17 (18, 19½, 21)"

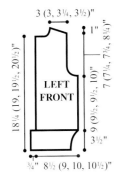

3 (3, 3¼, 3½)"
1"
18¼ (19, 19½, 20½)"
LEFT FRONT
7 (7¼, 7¾, 8¼)"
9 (9½, 9½, 10)"
3½"
¾"   8½ (9, 10, 10½)"

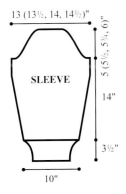

13 (13½, 14, 14½)"
5 (5½, 5¾, 6)"
SLEEVE
14"
3½"
10"

Color key
- ☐ Grey (MC)
- ◪ Aqua (A)
- ▲ Ruby (B)
- ◉ Olive (C)
- • Blue (D)
- ☒ Peach (E)
- ☑ Cranberry (F)
- − Med. Green (G)

— 12-st rep —

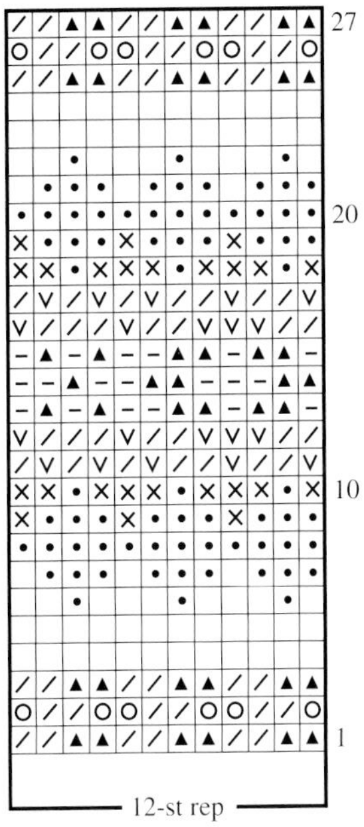

Women's Fall/Winter

Photo: Sante Forlano

A welcomed alternative to the tailored suit, this sophisticated cardigan looks office-smart paired with a knee-length skirt. We've updated the silhouette, added vents at the sides and cuffs, and given it a luxurious twist with an angora blend yarn. Shown in size Medium. The Tweedy Cardigan first appeared in the Fall/Winter 1958 issue of the original *Vogue Knitting* magazine.

Tweedy Cardigan

VERY EASY VERY VOGUE

SIZES
To fit X-Small (Small, Medium, Large, X-Large). Directions are for smallest size with larger sizes in parentheses. If there is only one figure, it applies to all sizes.

KNITTED MEASUREMENTS
● Bust (buttoned) 33½ (35, 37, 39¼, 40½)"/84 (87, 92, 98.5, 102.5)cm.
● Waist 32 (33, 35, 37¾, 39½)"/80 (83, 87, 94.5, 97.5)cm.
● Length 23 (23¼, 23½, 23¾, 24¼)"/58.5 (59, 59.5, 60, 61.5)cm.
● Upper arm 13 (13¼, 13½, 14½, 15½)"/33 (33.5, 34, 37, 39.5)cm.

MATERIALS
● 7 (8, 8, 9, 10) 1¾oz/50g balls (each approx 140yds/135m) of Tahki•Stacy Charles, Inc. *Sable* (wool/angora 4) in #1617 grey tweed
● One pair each sizes 5 and 8 (3.75 and 5mm) needles OR SIZE TO OBTAIN GAUGE
● Stitch holders
● Seven ⅞"/20mm buttons

Note
The original color used for this sweater is no longer available. A comparable color substitution has been made, which is available at the time of printing.

GAUGE
19 sts and 26 rows to 4"/10cm over pat st using size 8 (5mm) needles.
FOR PERFECT FIT, TAKE TIME TO CHECK GAUGE.

STITCH GLOSSARY
Pattern Stitch (multiple of 2 sts + 1)
Row 1 (RS) K1, *p1, k1; rep from * to end.
Row 2 Purl.
Rep these 2 rows for pat st.

BACK
With larger needles, cast on 79 (81, 85, 89, 93) sts. Work in pat st for 4"/10cm. Dec 1 st each side on next (RS) row and rep dec every 8th row 3 times more—71 (73, 77, 81, 85) sts. Work even until piece measures 9¼"/23.5cm from beg. Inc 1 st each side of next (RS) row and rep inc every 10th row 3 times more—79 (81, 85, 89, 93) sts. Work even until piece measures 15"/38cm from beg.

Armhole shaping
Bind off 5 (5, 5, 6, 6) sts at beg of next 2 rows. Dec 1 st each side every other row 3 (3, 4, 4, 5) times—63 (65, 67, 69, 71) sts. Work even until armhole measures 7 (7¼, 7½, 7¾, 8¼)"/18 (18.5, 19, 19.5, 21)cm.

Shoulder shaping
Bind off 6 sts at beg of next 6 (6, 4, 4, 2) rows, 7 sts at beg of next 0 (0, 2, 2, 4) rows. Bind off rem 27 (29, 29, 31, 31) sts for back neck.

LEFT FRONT
With larger needles, cast on 43 (45, 47, 51, 53) sts. Working the first 36 (38, 40, 44, 46) sts in pat st and the last 7 sts in k1, p1 rib (for front band), work side seam shaping at beg of RS rows as on back. There are 39 (41, 43, 47, 49) sts at waist and 43 (45, 47, 51, 53) sts at bust. Work even until piece measures 15"/38cm from beg.

Armhole shaping
Next row (RS) Bind off 5 (5, 5, 6, 6) sts, work to end. Dec 1 st at armhole edge every other row 3 (3, 4, 4, 5) times—35 (37, 38, 41, 42) sts. Work even until armhole measures 5¼ (5½, 5¾, 6, 6½)"/13.5 (14, 14.5, 15.5, 16.5)cm, end with a RS row.

Neck and shoulder shaping
Next row (WS) Sl first 7 sts to a holder, bind off 2 (2, 2, 3, 3) sts, work to end. Cont to shape neck, binding off 2 sts every other row 4 (5, 5, 6, 6) times. When same length as back, bind off 6 sts from shoulder edge 3 (3, 2, 2, 1) times, 7 sts 0 (0, 1, 1, 2) times.

RIGHT FRONT
Work to correspond to left front, reversing shaping and working 7 buttonholes, the first one at 2"/5cm from lower edge, the last one at ½"/1.25cm from top edge, and the others spaced evenly between as foll:
Buttonhole row (WS) Rib 3 sts, yo, k2tog, work to end.

SLEEVES

(**Note:** Sleeve length is planned for sleeve to be slightly long with slit, or to be folded back in a split cuff.)
With larger needles, cast on 39 (39, 39, 41, 41) sts. Work even in pat st for 2½"/6.5cm. Inc 1 st each side of next RS row and rep inc every 8th (8th, 6th, 6th, 6th) row 10 (11, 12, 13, 15) times more—61 (63, 65, 69, 73) sts. Work even until piece measures 18½"/47cm from beg.

Cap shaping

Bind off 5 (5, 5, 6, 6) sts at beg of next 2 rows. Dec 1 st each side every other row 15 (16, 17, 18, 20) times. Bind off 5 sts at beg of next 2 rows. Bind off rem 11 sts.

FINISHING

Block pieces to measurements. Sew shoulder seams. With smaller needles, pick up and k 92 (92, 92, 100, 100) sts evenly around neck edge, including sts from holders. P 1 row on WS, then p 1 row, k 1 row, p 1 row. Bind off. Roll edge to inside and sew. Leaving 3"/7.5cm free at lower edge, sew side seams. Leaving 2¼"/5.75cm free at cuff edge, sew sleeve seams. Set sleeves into armholes. Sew on buttons.

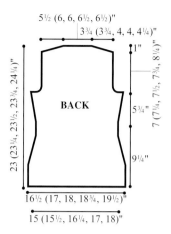

BACK

5½ (6, 6, 6½, 6½)"
3¾ (3¾, 4, 4, 4¼)"
1"
7 (7¼, 7½, 7¾, 8¼)"
5¾"
9¼"
23 (23¼, 23½, 23¾, 24¼)"
16½ (17, 18, 18¾, 19½)"
15 (15½, 16¼, 17, 18)"

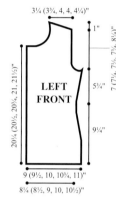

LEFT FRONT

3¼ (3¾, 4, 4, 4¼)"
1"
7 (7¼, 7½, 7¾, 8¼)"
5¾"
9¼"
20¼ (20½, 20¾, 21, 21½)"
9 (9½, 10, 10¾, 11)"
8¼ (8½, 9, 10, 10½)"

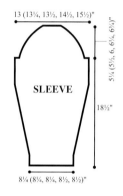

SLEEVE

13 (13¼, 13½, 14½, 15½)"
5¼ (5½, 6, 6¼, 6¾)"
18½"
8¼ (8¼, 8¼, 8½, 8½)"

Cabled A-Line Dress

This ribbed and cabled turtleneck knit dress features full-fashioned shaping for a sophisticated look. In place of the back neck zipper on the original, this updated version has a ribbed bodice for extra comfort and ease. Shown in size Small. The Cabled A-Line Dress first appeared in the Fall/Winter 1967 issue of the original *Vogue Knitting* magazine.

Photo: Alen MacWeeney

Cabled A-Line Dress

FOR INTERMEDIATE KNITTERS

SIZES
To fit Small (Medium, Large). Directions are for smallest size with larger sizes in parentheses. If there is only one figure, it applies to all sizes.

KNITTED MEASUREMENTS
- Bust 30 (34, 38)"/76 (86, 96.5)cm.
- Length 33¾ (34¾, 35½)"/85.5 (88, 90)cm.
- Upperarm 15¼ (16, 17)"/ 39 (40.5, 43)cm.

MATERIALS
- 18 (19, 19) 1¾oz/50g balls (each approx 100yds/90m) of Cleckheaton *Country Spun* by Plymouth (wool 3) in #1290 grey heather
- One pair each sizes 6 and 8 (4 and 5mm) needles OR SIZE TO OBTAIN GAUGE.
- Cable needle (cn)
- Size 6 (4mm) circular needle, 16"/40cm long
- Stitch markers

GAUGES
Note: Block swatch before determining gauge.
- 19 sts and 25 rows to 4"/10cm over St st using size 8 (5mm) needles.
- 20 sts to 3½"/9cm over chart pat using size 8 (5mm) needles.
- 28 sts and 26 rows to 4"/10cm over

k1, p1 rib using size 6 (4mm) needles (relaxed).
FOR PERFECT FIT, TAKE TIME TO CHECK GAUGES.

STITCH GLOSSARY
4-st Right Purl Cross (RPC) Sl 1 st to cn and hold to *back* of work, k3, p1 from cn.
4-st Left Purl Cross (LPC) Sl 3 sts to cn and hold to *front* of work, p1, k3 from cn.
6-st Right Cable (RC) Sl 3 sts to cn and hold to *back* of work, k3, k3 from cn.
Note: Work rows 1-34 of cable chart once, then rep rows 3-34.

BACK
With smaller needles, cast on 135 (143, 153) sts. Work in k1, p1 rib for 1"/2.5cm, dec 1 st on last WS row—134 (142, 152) sts. Change to larger needles.

Beg cable pat
Next row (RS) K21 (23, 25), *place marker (pm), work chart over next 20 sts, pm,* k52 (56, 62), rep between *'s once, k21 (23, 25). Cont in pats as established, working 20 sts between markers in cable pat (sl markers every row) and rem sts in St st, until 6 rows have been worked above rib.
Next row (RS) SSK (side dec), work to 2nd marker, k25 (27, 30), k2tog (center dec), work to last 2 sts, K2tog (side dec). Cont to dec 1 st at each side edge every 8th row 5 times more, every 10th row 8 times, AT SAME TIME, dec 1 st in center of piece every

6th row 7 times, every 8th row 10 times—88 (96, 106) sts. Work even until piece measures 22¾"/58cm from beg, end with chart row 8. K next row on RS, inc 17 (23, 27) sts evenly spaced across—105 (119, 133) sts. Change to smaller needles and work in k1, p1 rib for 1½ (2, 2½)"/4 (5, 6.5)cm, end with a WS row.

Armhole shaping
Next row (RS) K1, p1, SK2P, rib to last 5 sts, k3tog, p1, k1. Work row even. Rep last 2 rows twice more—93 (107, 121) sts. Work even in rib until armhole measures 8½ (9, 9¼)"/21.5 (23, 23.5)cm.

Shoulder shaping
Bind off 8 (10, 12) sts at beg of next 4 rows, 9 (11, 12) sts at beg of next 2 rows. Bind off rem 43 (45, 49) sts for back neck.

FRONT
Work as for back until armhole measures 7 (7½, 7¾)"/18 (19, 19.5)cm, end with a WS row.

Neck and shoulder shaping
Next row (RS) Work 38 (44, 49) sts, join 2nd ball of yarn and bind off 17 (19, 23) sts, work to end. Working both sides at once, bind off from each neck edge 3 sts twice, 2 sts 3 times, dec 1 st every other row once, AT THE SAME TIME, when same length as back to shoulders, shape shoulders as for back.

SLEEVES

With smaller needles, cast on 44 (48, 52) sts. Work in k1, p1 rib for 1"/2.5cm. Change to larger needles.

Beg cable pat

Next row (RS) K12 (14, 16) work row 9 of chart over next 20 sts, k12 (14, 16), Cont in pats as established, keeping center 20 sts in cable pat (work through row 34, then rep row 3-34) and rem sts in St st, inc 1 st each side (working inc sts into St st) [every 6th row once, every 8th row once] 8 times—76 (80, 84) sts. Work even until piece measures 20"/50.5cm from beg, end with chart row 30.

Cap shaping

Row 1 (RS) K2, SKP, work to last 4 sts, k2tog, k2. Row 2 P2, p2tog, work to last 4 sts, p2tog tbl, p2. Rep these 2 rows twice more. Bind off rem 64 (68, 72) sts.

FINISHING

Block pieces. Sew shoulder seams.

Neckband

With RS facing and circular needle, pick up and k100 (104, 112) sts evenly around neck edge. Join, pm and work in k1, p1 rib for 7"/18cm. Bind off loosely in rib. Set in sleeves. Sew side and sleeve seams.

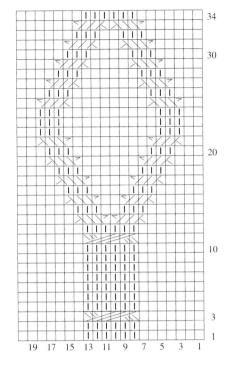

Stitch Key

- [I] k on RS, p on WS
- [ ] p on RS, k on WS
- [////] 4-st RPC
- [\\\\] 4-st LPC
- [\\////] 6-st RC

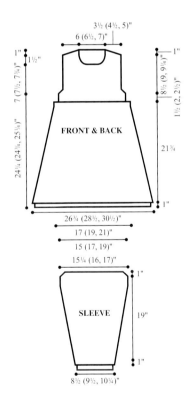

FRONT & BACK

SLEEVE

This roomy turtleneck combines the bulky stitches and bold shapes of the swinging '60s with the streamlined modernism of the 21st century. The generously scaled pullover boasts easy horseshoe cables with a fold-over funnel neck. Shown in size Medium. The Mohair Turtleneck first appeared in the Fall/Winter 1964 issue of the original *Vogue Knitting* magazine.

Mohair Turtleneck

VERY EASY VERY VOGUE

SIZES
To fit Small (Medium, Large). Directions are for smallest size with larger size in parentheses. If there is only one figure, it applies to all sizes.

KNITTED MEASUREMENTS
● Bust at underarm 41 (45½, 50)"/102 (113, 124)cm.
● Length 25½ (26, 26½)"/65 (66, 67)cm.
● Upper arm 16 (16½, 17)"/40 (41, 42)cm.

MATERIALS
Original Yarn
● 9 (10, 11) 1¾oz/50g balls (each approx 130yds/118m) of Bernat *Misti* (acrylic/mohair/ wool 4) in #14290 lilac
Substitute Yarn
● 9 (10, 11) 1¾oz/50g balls (each approx 136.5yds/125m) of Rowan Yarns *Kid Soft* (merino wool/kid mohair/ nylon 4) in #752 parma (lilac)
● One pair each sizes 10 and 10½ (6 and 7mm) needles OR SIZE TO OBTAIN GAUGE
● Size 10½ (7mm) circular needle, 16"/40cm long
● Stitch holders and cable needle (cn)

Note
The original yarn used for this sweater is no longer available. A comparable substitution has been made, which is available at the time of printing. Check gauge of substitute yarns very carefully before beginning.

GAUGE
18 sts and 18 rows to 4"/10cm over chart pat using size 10½ (7mm) needles. FOR PERFECT FIT, TAKE TIME TO CHECK GAUGE.

Note
To work gauge swatch, cast on 22 sts. Work 10-st rep twice, then work last 2 sts of chart. Work a total of 18 rows. Omitting first and last 2 sts, piece measures 4"/10cm square.

STITCH GLOSSARY
4-st Back Cable Sl 2 sts to cn and hold to *back*, k2, k2 from cn.
4-st Front Cable Sl 2 sts to cn and hold to *front*, k2, k2 from cn.

BACK
With size 10 (6mm) needles, cast on 82 (90, 100) sts. Work in k1, p1 rib for 1½"/4cm, inc 10 (12, 12) sts evenly across last row—92 (102, 112) sts. Change to larger needles.
Beg chart pat: Row 1 (RS) Work 10-st rep to last 2 sts, then work last 2 sts of chart. Cont in chart pat until piece measures 15½ (16, 16)"/39.5 (40.5, 40.5)cm from beg.

Armhole shaping
Bind off 5 (6, 6) sts at beg of next 2 rows. Dec 1 st each side every other row 5 times—72 (80, 90) sts. Work even until armhole measures 9 (9, 9½)"/23 (23, 24)cm, end with chart row 4 (2, 4).

Shoulder shaping
Bind off 7 (8, 11) sts at beg of next 2 rows, 8 (9, 11) sts at beg of next 2 rows. Place rem 42 (46, 46) sts on a holder for back neck.

FRONT
Work as for back until armhole measures 7¼ (7¼, 7¾)"/18.5 (18.5, 19.5)cm, end with chart row 4 (2, 4).

Neck shaping
Next row (RS) Work 20 (23, 28) sts, place center 32 (34, 34) sts on a holder, join 2nd ball of yarn and work to end. Working both sides at once, dec 1 st at each neck edge *every* row 5 (6, 6) times—15 (17, 22) sts each side. When same length as back to shoulder, shape shoulder as for back.

SLEEVES
With smaller needles, cast on 35 sts. Work in k1, p1 rib for 3"/7.5cm, inc 17 sts

evenly across last row—52 sts. Change to larger needles. Work in chart pat as for back, inc 1 st each side (working inc sts into pat) every 4th row 2 (4, 6) times, every 6th row 8 (7, 6) times—72 (74, 76) sts. Work even in pat until piece measures 16½ (17, 17½)"/41.5 (42.5, 43.5)cm from beg, end with a WS row.

Cap shaping

Bind off 5 (5, 6) sts at beg of next 2 rows, 3 sts at beg of next 4 rows, 2 sts at beg of next 4 rows. Dec 1 st each side every row 10 times, every other row 2 (2, 3) times. Bind off 2 sts at beg of next 4 rows. Bind off rem 10 (12, 10) sts.

FINISHING

Block pieces. Sew shoulder seams.

Funnel neck

With RS facing and circular needle, work in pat across 42 (46, 46) sts of back holder, pick up and k13 (10, 10) sts along left front neck edge, work pat across 32 (34, 34) sts of front neck, pick up and k13 (10, 10) sts along right front neck—100 sts. Join and cont in chart pat (reading all rows from right to left) for approx 4"/10cm, end with a chart row 4. P next rnd for turning ridge, dec 1 st in each p2 and 2 sts over each 8-st cable—70 sts. Cont in St st (k every rnd) for 4"/10cm more. Bind off. Fold band in half to WS at turning ridge and sew in place. Set in sleeves. Sew side and sleeve seams.

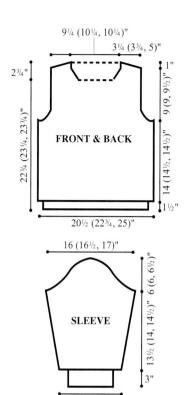

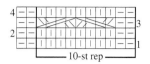

Stitch Key

☐ K on RS, p on WS

⊟ P on RS, k on WS

▨ 4-st BC

▧ 4-st FC

Button-Front Cardigan

This sleek little cardigan makes a light and chic winter-white chill chaser. It's close-fitting, with knit hems, pocket flaps, set-in sleeves, and a perfectly proportioned rib collar. Shown in size Medium. The Button-Front Cardigan first appeared in the Fall/Winter 1954 issue of the original *Vogue Knitting* magazine.

Photo: Sante Forlano

Button-Front Cardigan

FOR INTERMEDIATE KNITTERS

SIZES
To fit Small (Medium, Large, X-Large). Directions are for smallest size with larger sizes in parentheses. If there is only one figure, it applies to all sizes.

KNITTED MEASUREMENTS
● Bust (buttoned) 35 (37, 39, 41)"/89 (94, 99, 104)cm.
● Length 22½ (23, 23½, 24)"/57 (58.5, 59.5, 61)cm.
● Upper arm 12½ (13, 13½, 14)"/32 (33, 34, 35.5)cm.

MATERIALS
Original Yarn
● 9 (9, 10, 10) 1¾oz/50g balls (each approx 102yds/95m) of Cleckheaton *Wool Bouclé* by Plymouth (wool 5) in #1890 white
Substitute Yarn
● 10 (10, 11, 11) 1¾oz/50g balls (each approx 96yds/80m) of Brown Sheep Co. *Fantasy Lace* (wool 5) in #10 cream
● One pair size 8 (5mm) needles OR SIZE TO OBTAIN GAUGE
● Eight ¾"/20mm buttons
● Stitch holders

Note
The original yarn used for this sweater is no longer available. A comparable substitution has been made, which is available at the time of printing. Check gauge of substitute yarns very carefully before beginning.

GAUGE
16 sts and 24 rows to 4"/10cm over rev St st using size 8 (5mm) needles.
FOR PERFECT FIT, TAKE TIME TO CHECK GAUGE.

BACK
Cast on 70 (74, 78, 82) sts. Work in rev St st (p on RS, k on WS) until piece measures 14 (14, 14½, 14½)"/35.5 (35.5, 37, 37)cm from beg, end with a WS row.

Armhole shaping
Bind off 5 sts at beg of next 2 rows. Dec 1 st each side on next row, then every other row 2 (3, 3, 4) times more—54 (56, 60, 62) sts. Work even until armhole measures 7½ (8, 8, 8½)"/19 (20.5, 20.5, 21.5)cm, end with a WS row.

Shoulder shaping
Bind off 6 (6, 7, 7) sts at beg of next 4 rows, then 6 (7, 6, 6) sts at beg of next 2 rows. Bind off rem 18 (18, 20, 22) sts.

POCKET FLAPS (make 2)
Cast on 19 sts. Beg with a WS row, work 3 rows in rev St st.
Next row (RS) P8, bind off 3 sts, p8.
Next row K8, cast on 3 sts over bound-off sts, k8. Work 2 rows even. Place sts on a holder.

LEFT FRONT
Cast on 45 (47, 49, 51) sts.
Row 1 (RS) P4, [k1, p1] 9 times, k1, p15 (17, 19, 21), k1, p6.
Row 2 K6, wyif sl 1, k15 (17, 19, 21), work rib over 19 sts, k4. Cont in pat as established until piece measures 4½"/11.5cm from beg, end with a WS row.
Next row P4, bind off 19 sts, work to end.
Next row Work to bound-off sts, k19 sts from pocket flap holder, k4.
Next row (RS) P to last 7 sts, k1, p6.
Work even until piece measures same as back to armhole, end with a WS row. Shape armhole at beg of RS rows as for back—37 (38, 40, 41) sts. Work even until armhole measures 5½ (6, 6, 6½)"/14 (15, 15, 16.5)cm, end with a RS row.

Neck shaping
Next row (WS) Bind off 15 (15, 16, 17) sts (neck edge) k to end. Cont to bind off at neck edge 2 sts twice. Work even until same length as back to shoulder shaping. Shape shoulder at beg of RS rows as for back. Place markers along left front edge for 6 buttons, with the first 1"/2.5cm from lower edge, the last ½"/1.25cm from neck edge, and 4 others spaced evenly between.

RIGHT FRONT
Work as for left front, reversing shaping and pocket placement. Work double buttonholes opposite button markers of left front as foll:

Next row (RS) P2, bind off 2 sts, p2, k1, p2, bind off 2 sts, work to end; on next row, cast on 2 sts over each pair of bound-off sts.

SLEEVES

Cast on 40 (42, 44, 44) sts. Work in rev St st, inc 1 st each side every 16th (16th, 16th, 14th) row 5 (5, 5, 6) times—50 (52, 54, 56) sts. Work even until piece measures 15"/38cm from beg, end with a WS row.

Cap shaping

Bind off 5 sts at beg of next 2 rows. Work 2 rows even. Dec 1 st each side on next row, then every 4th row 4 times more, then every other row 6 (7, 8, 9) times. Work 1 row even. Bind off 2 sts at beg of next 6 rows. Bind off rem 6 sts.

FINISHING

Block pieces to measurements. Sew shoulder seams. Fold front facings to WS at sl st and sew in place. Work buttonhole st around buttonholes.

Collar

Cast on 81 (81, 85, 89) sts. Work in k1, p1 rib for 3½"/9cm. Bind off loosely in rib. Sew collar in place around neck edge, beg and end 1½"/4cm in from each front edge.

Pocket linings (make 2)

Cast on 19 sts. Work in rev St st until piece measures 3½"/9cm. Bind off. Sew in place on WS. Set in sleeves. Sew side and sleeve seams. Sew 1 button on each pocket. Sew rem buttons on left front edge.

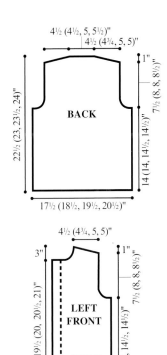

4½ (4½, 5, 5½)"
4½ (4¾, 5, 5)"
1"
7½ (8, 8, 8½)"
22½ (23, 23½, 24)"
BACK
14 (14, 14½, 14½)"
17½ (18½, 19½, 20½)"

12½ (13, 13½, 14)"
6¾ (7, 7½, 7¾)"
SLEEVE
15"
10 (10½, 11, 11)"

4½ (4¾, 5, 5)"
3"
1"
7½ (8, 8, 8½)"
19½ (20, 20½, 21)"
LEFT FRONT
14 (14, 14½, 14½)"
1½" 9½ (10, 10½, 11)"

This classically elegant, figure-flattering sweater is as irresistible now as it was back in the Fifties. Semi-fitted, the cardigan jacket has alternating cable and stockinette stitch panels, set-in sleeves, crochet edging, and an optional knitted belt. Shown in size Small. The Belted Cardigan first appeared in the Fall/Winter 1952 issue of the original *Vogue Knitting* magazine.

Belted Cardigan

FOR INTERMEDIATE KNITTERS

SIZES
To fit Small (Medium, Large, X-Large). Directions are for smallest size with larger sizes in parentheses. If there is only one figure, it applies to all sizes.

KNITTED MEASUREMENTS
- Bust (closed) 36 (38, 40, 42)"/ 91.5 (96.5, 101.5, 106.5)cm.
- Length 22½ (23½, 24, 25)"/57.5 (60, 61, 63.5)cm.
- Length of sleeve to underarm 17½ (17½, 18, 18)"/44.5 (44.5, 46, 46)cm.

MATERIALS
Original Yarn
- 8 (9, 10, 11) 1¾oz/50g balls (each approx 126yds/115m) of Pingouin *France +* (wool/acrylic 4) in #0096 coral

Substitute Yarn
- 8 (9, 10, 11) 1¾/50g balls (each approx 132yds/120m) of Baruffa *7 Settembre* (wool 4) in #8523 coral
- One pair size 6 (4mm) needles OR SIZE TO OBTAIN GAUGE
- Size F (4.00mm) crochet hook
- 6⅝"/1.5mm buttons
- Yarn needle
- Cable needle (cn)

Optional Knitted Belt:
- 1 circular (or desired shape) buckle with 2"/5cm center bar
- Inner belt facing (to fit waist measurement plus 6"/15cm)

Note
The original yarn used for this sweater is no longer available. A comparable substitution has been made, which is available at the time of printing. Check gauge of substitute yarns very carefully before beginning.

GAUGE
23 sts and 30 rows to 5"/3.75cm over St st using size 6 (4mm) needles. FOR PERFECT FIT, TAKE TIME TO CHECK GAUGE.

STITCH GLOSSARY
4-st Back Cable (BC)
Row 1 (RS) K4.
Row 2 (WS) P4.
Row 3 (RS) Sl 2 sts to cn and hold to *back* of work, k2, k2 from cn.
Rows 5, 7 (RS) K4.
Row 4, 6 and 8 (WS) P4.
Rows 9-14 Rep rows 3-8.
Rows 15 and 16 Rep rows 3 and 4.

BACK
Cast on 102 (108, 116, 126) sts.
Beg cable band: Row 1 (RS) P1 (4, 8, 1), *k4, p8; rep from *, end k4, p1 (4, 8, 1).
Row 2 K1 (4, 8, 1), *p4, k8; rep from *, end p4, k1 (4, 8, 1).
Row 3 P1 (4, 8, 1), *BC, p8; rep from *, end k4, p1 (4, 8, 1). Work rows 4-16, in pat as established with BC cable twists on rows 9 and 15 (end on WS with row 16).
Beg St st band: Row 1 (RS) Work in St

st for 12 rows, end WS row. Cont alternating band pats until piece measures 14½ (15, 15½, 16)"/37 (38, 39, 40.5)cm, end with WS row.

Armhole shaping
Bind off 8 sts beg next 2 rows. Dec 1 st each side every other row 4 (4, 5, 6) times—78 (84, 90, 98) sts. Work even until armhole measures 7½ (8, 8, 8½)"/19 (20.5, 20.5, 21.5)cm, end with WS row.

Shoulder shaping
Bind off 12 (13, 14, 15) sts beg next 4 (2, 2, 2) rows, bind off 0 (12, 13, 14) at beg of next 0 (2, 2, 2) rows. Bind off rem 30 (34, 36, 40) sts from back neck.

LEFT FRONT
Cast on 57 (60, 64, 70) sts.
Beg cable band: Row 1 (RS) P1 (4, 8, 2), work in pat as for back, ending with p4 (front edge). Work even in est pat until same length as back to underarm. Shape armhole at side edge (beg of RS row) as for back. Work even until armhole measures 5" (12.5cm), end with RS row.

Neck shaping
Next row (WS) Bind off 7 (9, 10, 13) sts knitwise (neck edge) work to end. Cont to bind off 2 sts at neck edge every other row 7 times. When same length as back to shoulders, shape shoulder at side edge as for back.

RIGHT FRONT

Work to correspond to left front, reversing shaping. Place six markers for buttonloops as foll: first 1"/2.5cm from the neckline, second 1"/2.5cm from bottom. Space 4 rem evenly between.

SLEEVES

(**Note:** In order for sleeve to match fronts/back, end sleeve pat at same sequence as sweater to underarm shaping, end with WS row.)
Cast on 54 (54, 56, 58) sts.
Beg cable band: Row 1 (RS) P1 (1, 2, 3), *k4, p8; rep from *, end k4, p1 (1, 2, 3). Starting with row 19, inc 1 st each side on next and every 8th row 8 (9, 9, 10) times more—72 (74, 76, 80) sts. Work even until piece measures 17½ (17½, 18, 18½)"/44.5 (44.5, 46, 47)cm from beg.

Cap shaping

With RS facing, bind 8 sts beg next 2 rows, then dec 1 st each side every other row 4 times, every 4th row 3 times, every other row 10 times. Bind off rem 22 (24, 26, 30) sts.

FINISHING

Block pieces to measurements. Sew shoulder seams. Set in sleeves. Sew side and sleeve seams.

Border

With RS facing, attach yarn to lower right-hand side seam. Work 1 row of sc around all edges, working 2 sc in corners (all rows to keep work flat), sl st in first sc. Work 1 sc in each sc, working up right front edge work to within 1 sc of marker, ch 3, skip 3 sc's, cont around in established pat, sl st in 2 first sc. Work sc in each sc and 1 sc in each ch st around in pat, sl st in first sc. Fasten off. Work 3 rows of sc around bottom of sleeves. Sew on buttons.

BELT (optional)

Draw a center line on belt facing. To form pointed belt end, measure 1½"/3.8cm down, mark at side edges. With a ruler, draw diagonal lines from side edges up to center point. To form curved belt end, measure 1"/2.5cm down on center line and mark. Place compass point on mark and draw a half circle for the curve. Cut.
Cast on 24 sts. Work in St st until desired length to beg of point or curved shaping.
Row 1 (RS) Knit.

Row 2 Purl. Work in St st until desired length to beg of point or curved shaping, end on P side.

Belt end shaping

Row 1 K5, sl 2tog as to k, k next st, pass 2 slip sts over, (double decrease made—S2KP) k to last 8 sts, S2KP, k5.
Row 2 Purl.
Row 3 K4, S2KP, k to last 7 sts, S2KP, k4.
Row 4 (**Note:** For curved-tip belt, bind off on this row.) Purl.
Row 5 K3, S2KP, k to last 6 sts, S2KP, k3. Cont as established in dec pat until 2 sts rem.
Next row P2tog. Bind off.

Crocheted-covered buckle

With hook and sc, attach slip knot to buckle. Working around buckle edge, draw up a lp, yo, pull yarn through 2 lp, cont around keeping sts close tog. Fasten off. Tuck in yarn ends.

Assemble

Lay belt facing on WS of work, secure with thread at ends. Using center guide line and yarn needle, sew back seam. Fold straight edge of belt end over buckle bar, sew in place. Steam lightly on both sides according to yarn directions.

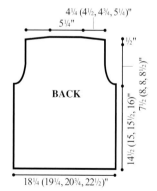

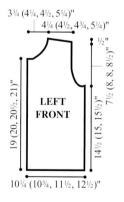

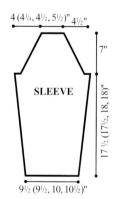

Woven-Stitch Jacket

With its incredible all-over lattice cable stitch patterning, this zip-front jacket is as fashion-right today as it was when it first appeared in the '60s. The jacket has set in sleeves, side-slit pockets, and a crocheted edging for a neat finish. Shown in size Medium. The Woven-Stitch Jacket first appeared in the Fall/Winter 1969 issue of the original *Vogue Knitting* magazine.

Woven-Stitch Jacket

FOR INTERMEDIATE KNITTERS

SIZES
To fit Small (Medium, Large, X-Large). Directions are for smallest size with larger sizes in parentheses. If there is only one figure, it applies to all sizes.

KNITTED MEASUREMENTS
● Bust (closed) 39 (42, 44, 47)"/99 (106.5, 111.5, 119)cm.
● Length 26½ (27½, 28, 28½)"/67.5 (70, 71, 72.5)cm.
● Upper arm 14½ (16, 16, 17)"/37 (42, 42, 43)cm.

MATERIALS
● 14 (15, 17, 19) 3½oz/100g balls (each approx 183yds/167m) of GGH/Muench Yarns *Sportivo* (wool 5) in #20 lt teal
● One pair each sizes 10 and 11 (6 and 8mm) needles OR SIZE TO OBTAIN GAUGE
● Cable needle (cn)
● Crochet hook size H/8 (5.00mm)
● One 23 (24, 24, 25)"/58.5 (61, 61, 63.5)cm zipper (matching color)
● 1yd/1m matching lining materials (for pocket linings)
● Matching thread

GAUGE
24 sts and 23 rows to 5"/12.5cm over cable pat st using size 11 (8mm) needles.
FOR PERFECT FIT, TAKE TIME TO CHECK GAUGE.

STITCH GLOSSARY
Cable Pat (multiple of 6 sts)
Rows 1 and 3 (WS) Purl.
Row 2 and 6 (RS) Knit.
Row 4 K3, *sl next 3 sts to cn and hold to *back,* k3, k3 from cn; rep from * end k3.
Rows 5 and 7 Purl.
Row 8 *Sl next 3 sts to cn and hold to *front,* k3, k3 from cn; rep from * to end.
Rep rows 1-8 for cable pat st.

Gauge swatch
With larger needles, cast on 28 sts.
Row 1 (WS) K2 (selvage sts), p24, k2 (selvage sts).
Row 2 (RS) P2 (selvage sts), k24, p2 (selvage sts). Cont in pat st with selvage sts for 23 rows. Swatch should measure 5"/12.5cm square, not including selvage sts.

BACK
With smaller needles, cast on 94 (100, 106, 112) sts.
Row 1 (WS) K2, p90 (96, 102, 108), k2. Change to larger needles and cont in pat st, with 2 reverse St st selvage sts each side, until piece measures 17½ (18, 18, 18)"/44.5 (45.5, 45.5, 45.5)cm from beg.

Armhole shaping
Bind off 3 sts at beg of next 2 rows.
Next row (RS) P2, k2tog (for 1 st dec), work pat to last 4 sts, k2tog, p2. Cont with p2 selvage sts each side as before, dec 1 st each side every other row 2 (2,

5, 5) times more—82 (88, 88, 94) sts. Work even in pat st until armhole measures 7½ (8, 8½, 9)"/19 (20.5, 21.5, 23)cm.

Shoulder shaping
(**Note:** While binding off sts, to keep edge from rippling, work as foll: *bind off 2 sts, then k2tog and bind off; rep from * for all bound-off edges.) Bind off 8 (9, 9, 10) sts at beg of next 6 rows. Bind off rem 34 sts for back neck.

LEFT FRONT
With smaller needles, cast on 52 (58, 58, 64) sts.
Row 1 (WS) K2, p48 (54, 54, 60), k2. Change to larger needles and cont in pat st, with 2 reverse St st selvage sts each side, until piece measures 3"/7.5cm from beg, end with a WS row.

Pocket opening
Next row (RS) Work 14 (14, 14, 20) sts, join 2nd ball of yarn and work to end. Cont to work both sides with separate balls of yarn for 6½"/16.5cm from beg of pocket opening. Cut extra ball of yarn and work across all sts with single ball of yarn until piece measures 17½ (18, 18, 18)"/44.5 (45.5, 45.5, 45.5)cm from beg.

Armhole shaping
Bind off 3 sts from beg of next RS row (armhole edge), then resuming p2 selvage sts, dec 1 st inside of selvage sts every other row 3 (3, 3, 6) times—46

(52, 52, 55) sts. Work even until armhole measures 5½ (6, 6½, 7)"/14 (15.5, 16.5, 18)cm, end with a RS row.

Neck shaping
Next row (WS) Bind off 9 (12, 12, 12) sts, work to end. Cont to bind off 3 sts from neck edge every other row 3 times, dec 1 st every other row 4 times—24 (27, 27, 30) sts. When same length as back to shoulder, shape shoulder as for back.

RIGHT FRONT
Work as for left front, reversing all shaping and placing pocket opening at 38 (44, 44, 44) sts from center front.

SLEEVES
With smaller needles, cast on 52 sts.
Row 1 (WS) K2, p48, k2. Change to larger needles and cont in pat st, with 2 reverse St st selvage sts each side, until piece measures 2½"/6.5cm from beg.

Next row (RS) P2, inc 1 st in next st, work to last 3 sts, inc 1 st in next st, p2. Cont to work incs in this way (working cable twists when there are sufficient sts in pat) every 4th row 8 (11, 11, 14) times more— 70 (76, 76, 82) sts. Work even in pat until piece measures 17"/43cm from beg.

Cap shaping
(**Note:** When binding off sts, cont to make cable twists of 2 over 2, or 2 over 1, or 1 over 1 to keep neatness of pattern at sleeve cap edges.) Discontinue selvage sts and bind off 3 sts at beg of next 8 (10, 2, 4) rows, bind off 2 sts at beg of next 10 (10, 22, 22) rows. Bind off rem 26 sts.

Collar
With smaller needles, cast on 110 sts.
Row 1 (WS) K1, p108, k1. Having only one p selvage st each side, work in pat st for 4 rows. Change to larger needles and cont in pat st until collar measures 3½"/9cm, end with pat row 1. Bind off.

FINISHING
Block pieces to measurements. For pocket linings, cut 2 lining pieces 14" x 7½"/35.5cm x 19cm from fabric. Fold in half (to square off) and take a ½"/1.25cm seam on each edge, leaving opening for pocket opening. Take ½"/1.25cm seam at top of lining. Tack pocket linings to inside of jacket. Sew shoulder seams. Sew sleeves into armholes. Sew side and sleeve seams. With RS facing and crochet hook, work 60 sc around neck edge. Ch 1, turn. Work 1 sc in each sc. Work 60 sc along cast-on edge of collar and sew this edge to neck edge. Work sc evenly along cuff edges, ch 1, do not turn, but work 1 backwards sc (working from left to right) in each sc. Work sc and backwards sc edge along lower and center front edges, around outer edges of collar and around pocket opening. Tack zipper in place, then baste carefully. Sew zipper to inside edge, reinforcing at top and lower edges.

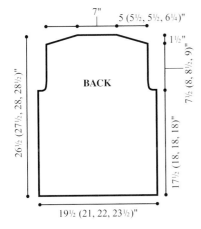

BACK

26½ (27½, 28, 28½)"

19½ (21, 22, 23½)"

7"

5 (5½, 5½, 6¼)"

1½"

7½ (8, 8½, 9)"

17½ (18, 18, 18)"

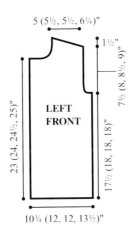

LEFT FRONT

23 (24, 24½, 25)"

10¾ (12, 12, 13½)"

5 (5½, 5½, 6¼)"

1½"

7½ (8, 8½, 9)"

17½ (18, 18, 18)"

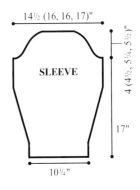

SLEEVE

14½ (16, 16, 17)"

4 (4½, 5¼, 5½)"

17"

10¾"

Jumbo-sized needles and a lofty yarn make this striking Aran fun and fast to knit. While the color and proportions have been updated, everything else remains the same as the original. Shown in size Medium. The Chunky Aran first appeared in the Spring/Summer 1968 issue of the original *Vogue Knitting* magazine.

Chunky Aran

VERY EASY VERY VOGUE

SIZES
To fit Small (Medium, Large, X-Large). Directions are for smallest size with larger sizes in parentheses. If there is only one figure, it applies to all sizes.

KNITTED MEASUREMENTS
● Bust 38 (40, 44, 46)"/96.5 (101.5, 111.5, 117)cm.
● Length 23½ (23½, 24, 24½)"/59.5 (59.5, 61, 62)cm.
● Upper arm 15½ (15½, 17, 18)"/39.5 (39.5, 43, 45.5)cm.

MATERIALS
● 6 (6, 7, 7) 8oz/250g skeins (each approx 310yds/286m) of Wool Pak Yarns NZ/Baabajoes Wool Company *14 Ply* (wool 6) in tussock
● One pair each sizes 17 and 19 (12.75 and 16mm) needles
● Cable needle (cn)

GAUGE
7 sts and 10 rows to 4"/10cm over seed st using 3 strands of yarn and size 19 (16mm) needles. FOR PERFECT FIT, TAKE TIME TO CHECK GAUGE.

Notes
1 Work with 3 strands of yarn held tog throughout.
2 Make a test swatch using 3 strands of yarn and size 19 (16mm) needles.

Since needle substitution is not a possibility, simply work more tightly or loosely to achieve given gauge.

STITCH GLOSSARY
Seed Stitch
Row 1 (RS) *K1, p1; rep from * to end.
Row 2 K the purl sts and p the knit sts.
Rep row 2 for seed st.

Cable Pattern (over 4 sts)
Row 1 (RS) P1, k2, p1.
Row 2 K1, p2, k1.
Row 3 P1, sl next st to cn and hold to *front*, k1, k1 from cn, p1.
Row 4 Rep row 2.
Rep rows 1-4 for cable pat.

RPT
Sl 1 st to cn and hold to *back*, k1 tbl, p1 from cn.
LPT
Sl 1 st to cn and hold to *front*, p1, k1 tbl, from cn.
3-st LPT
Sl 2 sts to cn and hold to *front*, k1 tbl, work k1 tbl, p1 from cn.

BACK
With smaller needles and 3 strands of yarn held tog, cast on 31 (33, 37, 39) sts.
Row 1 (RS) K1 tbl, *p1, k1 tbl; rep from * to end.
Row 2 P1 tbl, *k1, p1 tbl; rep from * to end. Rep these 2 rows for twisted rib 3 times more. Change to larger needles.

Beg pats
Row 1 (RS) Work 5 (6, 8, 9) sts in seed st, 4 sts in cable pat, 13 sts in diamond pat foll chart row 1, 4 sts in cable pat, 5 (6, 8, 9) sts in seed st. Cont in pats as established, working through row 26 of chart, then rep rows 3-26 of chart until piece measures 16"/40.5cm from beg.

Armhole shaping
Bind off 2 sts at beg of next 2 rows. Dec 1 st each side of next row and every other row 1 (1, 2, 2) times more—23 (25, 27, 29) sts. Work even until armhole measures 7½ (7½, 8, 8½)"/19 (19, 20.5, 21.5)cm.

Shoulder shaping
Bind off 6 (7, 7, 8) sts at beg of next 2 rows. Bind off rem 11 (11, 13, 13) sts for back neck.

FRONT
Work as for back until armhole measures 6½ (6½, 7, 7½)"/16.5 (16.5, 18, 19)cm.

Neck shaping
Next row (RS) Work 7 (8, 8, 9) sts, join another 3 strands of yarn and bind off center 9 (9, 11, 11) sts, work to end. Working both sides at once, dec 1 st from each neck edge on next row. When same length as back, bind off rem 6 (7, 7, 8) sts each side for shoulders.

SLEEVES
With smaller needles and 3 strands of

yarn held tog, cast on 15 (15, 17, 17) sts. Work 8 rows twisted rib as for back. Change to larger needles.

Beg pats
Row 1 (RS) Work 1 (1, 2, 2) sts in seed st, 13 sts in diamond pat foll row 1 of chart, 1 (1, 2, 2) sts in seed st. Cont in pats, inc 1 st each side (working inc sts in seed st) every 6th row 5 (5, 5, 3) times, every 4th row 0 (0, 0, 3) times— 25 (25, 27, 29) sts. Work even until piece measures 16½"/42cm from beg.

Cap shaping
Bind off 2 sts at beg of next 2 rows. Dec 1 st each side of next row then every other row 1 (1, 2, 3) times more—

17 sts. Work even for 5 (5, 4, 3) rows more. Bind off.

FINISHING
Block pieces to measurements. Sew shoulder seams. Sew sleeves into armholes. Sew side and sleeve seams.

Bias neckband
With smaller needles and 3 strands of yarn held tog, cast on 5 sts.
Row 1 (RS) K1 tbl, *p1, k1 tbl; rep from * once.
Row 2 Work 2 sts tog, work twisted rib to last st, inc 1 st in rib in last st. Work 1 row even. Rep last 2 rows for bias neckband until piece fits around entire neck edge. Leave sts on a holder and

sew one long edge around neck (so that neckband sits up from neck as in photo). Adjust length if necessary, then bind off sts. Sew ends of neckband tog.

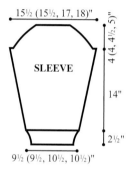

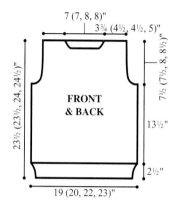

Stitch Key
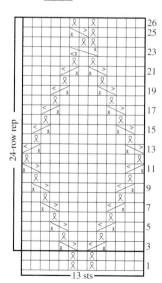

Chunky Turtleneck

Large needles and multiple strands of yarn make this ultra-chic turtleneck super quick to make. The ribbed pullover features fully-fashioned raglan sleeves and a comfy, loose fit. Shown in size Medium. The Chunky Turtleneck first appeared in the Fall 1968 issue of the original *Vogue Knitting* magazine.

VERY EASY VERY VOGUE

Chunky Turtleneck

SIZES
To fit Small (Medium, Large, X-Large). Directions are for smallest size with larger sizes in parentheses. If there is only one figure, it applies to all sizes.

KNITTED MEASUREMENTS
● Bust 42 (45, 49, 52½)"/106.5 (114, 124.5, 133)cm.
● Length 25¾ (26, 27¼, 28)"/65.5 (66, 69, 71)cm.
● Upper arm 16 (17½, 21, 21)"/40.5 (44.5, 53, 53)cm.

MATERIALS
Original Yarn
● 10 (10, 12, 14) 1¾oz/50g balls (each approx 107yds/98m) of Lion Brand Yarns AL•PA•KA (acrylic/ wool/alpaca 3) in #149 silver grey (A)
● 12 (12, 14, 16) balls in #249 grey tweed (B)
Substitute Yarn
● 10 (10, 12, 14) 1¾oz/50g balls (each approx 110yds/101m) of Cleckheaton/Plymouth Yarns Country 8 Ply Naturals (wool/acrylic/nylon 4) in #149 silver grey (A)
● 18 (19, 19) skeins in #1827 grey mix
● One pair size 19 (16mm) needles OR SIZE TO OBTAIN GAUGE
● Size 19 (16mm) circular needle, 24"/60cm long

Note
The original yarn used for this sweater is no longer available. A comparable substitution has been made, which is available at the time of printing. Check gauge of substitute yarns very carefully before beginning.

GAUGE
7 sts and 10 rows to 4"/10cm over k2, p1 rib using 4 strands of yarn and size 19 (16mm) needles. FOR PERFECT FIT, TAKE TIME TO CHECK GAUGE.

STITCH GLOSSARY
K2, P1 Rib
(multiple of 3 sts + 1)
Row 1 (RS) P1, *k2, p1; rep from * to end.
Row 2 K1, *p2, k1; rep from * to end.
Rep rows 1 and 2 for k2, p1 rib.

BACK
With 2 strands A held tog with 2 strands B, cast on 37 (40, 43, 46) sts. Work in k2, p1 rib for 17 (16½, 16, 16)"/43 (42, 40.5, 40.5)cm.

Raglan armhole shaping
Bind off 3 sts at beg of next 2 rows.
Dec row (RS) P1, k1, ssk, rib to last 4 sts, k2tog, k1, p1.
Next row K1, p2, rib to last 3 sts, p2, k1. Rep last 2 rows 8 (9, 11, 12) times more—13 (14, 13, 14) sts. Bind off.

FRONT
Work as for back to armhole.

Raglan armhole shaping
Bind off 3 sts at beg of next 2 rows.
Dec row 1 (RS) P1, k1, sssk (for dec 2 sts), rib to last 5 sts, k3tog (for dec 2 sts), k1, p1.
Next row K1, p2, rib to last 3 sts, p2, k1. Rep last 2 rows once more.
Dec row 2 (RS) P1, k1, ssk, rib to last 4 sts, k2tog, k1, p1.
Next row K1, p2 rib to last 3 sts, p2, k1. Rep last 2 rows 4 (5, 7, 8) times more— 13 (14, 13, 14) sts. Bind off.

LEFT SLEEVE
With 2 strands A held tog with 2 strands B, cast on 16 (19, 19, 19) sts. Work in k2, p1 rib, inc 1 st each side every 6th row 2 (2, 1, 1) times, every 4th row 4 (4, 8, 8) times—28 (31, 37, 37) sts. Work even until piece measures 16½"/42cm from beg.

Raglan cap shaping
Bind off 3 sts at beg of next 2 rows.
Dec row (RS) P1, k1, ssk, rib to last 4 sts, k2tog, k1, p1.
Next row K1, p2, rib to last 3 sts, p2, k1. Rep last 2 rows 6 (7, 9, 10) times more—8 (9, 11, 9) sts.
Next row (RS) P1, k1, ssk, rib to end.
Next row (WS) Bind off 3 (3, 4, 3) sts, work to end.
Next row P1, k1, ssk, rib to end, sl last st. Bind off 3 (4, 5, 4) sts.

RIGHT SLEEVE
Work to correspond to left sleeve, reversing shaping at top of cap (by

binding off at beg of RS rows and dec sts end of RS rows).

FINISHING
Block pieces to measurements. Sew raglan sleeves into armholes.

Turtleneck
With circular needle and 4 strands of yarn (2A, 2B), picking up in back lps only of bound-off sts, pick up and k 39 (42, 39, 42) sts evenly around neck edge. Join.
Rnd 1 *P1, k2; rep from * around. Rep this rnd until turtleneck measures 3¼"/8.5cm. K next rnd for turning ridge.
Next rnd *K1, p2; rep from * around. Rep this rnd until turtleneck measures 7"/18cm. Bind off in rib. Sew side and sleeve seams.

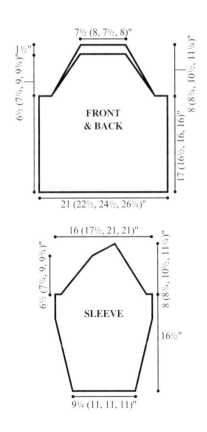

Incredibly cozy and warm, this chunky coat was knit directly from the original pattern—only the yarn has changed. Worked in stockinette with a wonderfully textural border, it's quick to knit on giant-sized needles. Shown in size Medium. The Chunky Coat first appeared in the Spring/Summer 1968 issue of the original *Vogue Knitting* magazine.

Chunky Coat

VERY EASY VERY VOGUE

SIZES
To fit Small (Medium, Large). Directions are for smallest size with larger sizes in parentheses. If there is only one figure, it applies to all sizes.

KNITTED MEASUREMENTS
● Bust (wrapped) 37 (40, 42)"/94 (101.5, 106.5)cm.
● Length 38 (39, 40)"/96.5 (99, 101.5)cm.
● Upper arm 16 (17½, 19½)"/40.5 (44.5, 49.5)cm.

MATERIALS
● 23 (24, 26) 1¾oz/50g balls (each approx 39yds/35m) of Filatura Di Crosa/Tahki•Stacy Charles, Inc. *Muschio* (alpaca/wool/acrylic/polyamide 5) in #356 grey (A)
● 7 (7, 8) 1¾oz/50g balls (each approx 154yds/140m) of *Ultralight* (alpaca/wool/nylon 5) in #1 grey (B)
● 5 (5, 6) 1¾oz/50g balls (each approx 136.5yds/125m) of *Zara* (wool 3) in #1494 grey (C)
● One pair size 35 (19mm) needles
● Three large coat hook-and-eye sets
● ½yd/.5m of textured weft fusible interfacing
● 1 large novelty button
● Size Q (16mm) crochet hook

GAUGE
9 sts and 14 rows to 8"/20cm over St st using 5 strands of yarn and size 35 (19mm) needles. FOR PERFECT FIT, TAKE TIME TO CHECK GAUGE.

Note
Make a test swatch using 2 strands A, 2 strands B and 1 strand C (5 strands of yarn) held tog. Since needle substitution is not a possibility, simply work more tightly or loosely to achieve given gauge.

BACK
With 2 strands A, 2 strands B and 1 strand C (5 strands of yarn) held tog, cast on 20 (22, 24) sts. Work in reverse St st (p 1 row, k 1 row) for 8 rows. Then work in St st until piece measures 28"/71cm from beg, end with a WS row.

Raglan armhole shaping
Bind off 2 sts at beg of next 2 rows. Work even for 2 rows. Dec 1 st each side of next row. Work 1 row even. Rep last 2 rows 4 (5, 6) times more. Bind off rem 6 sts.

LEFT FRONT
With 5 strands of yarn, cast on 10 (12, 14) sts. Work as for back to armholes.

Raglan armhole shaping
Next row (RS) Bind off 2 sts, work to end. Work even for 3 rows. Dec 1 st at armhole edge on next row then every

other row 4 (5, 6) times more—3 (4, 5) sts. Bind off on next WS row.

RIGHT FRONT
With 5 strands of yarn, cast on 16 (18, 20) sts. Work in reverse St st for 8 rows.
Next row (RS) P7 (front border), k9 (11, 13). Keeping the first 7 sts in reverse St st for front border and rem sts in St st, work as for left front, reversing raglan shaping. Bind off rem 9 (10, 11) sts when armhole shaping is completed.

SLEEVES
With 5 strands of yarn, cast on 14 (16, 18) sts. Work in reverse St st for 8 rows. Then work in St st for 2 rows. Inc 1 st each side of next row, then every 8th row once more—18 (20, 22) sts. Work even until piece measures 18"/45.5cm from beg.

Raglan cap shaping
Work as for back. Bind off rem 4 sts.

COLLAR
With 5 strands of yarn, cast on 30 (32, 34) sts. [K 1 row, p 1 row] twice. Bind off loosely.

FINISHING
Block pieces lightly to measurements. Cut fusible fabric to line collar. Following manufacturer's directions, fuse to WS of collar. With single strand of yarn, sew raglan sleeves into raglan armholes. Sew side and sleeve seams. Sew collar around neck edge. With crochet hook

and 5 strands of yarn, work an edge of
sc along fronts and all around collar.
Sew button to left collar and pull through
sc edge. Sew on hook-and-eye closures
to collar and along fronts.

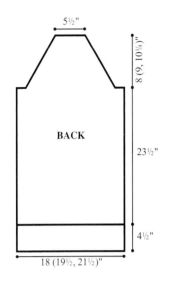

5½"

8 (9, 10¼)"

BACK

23½"

4½"

18 (19½, 21½)"

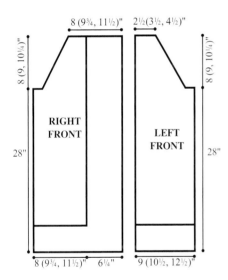

8 (9¾, 11½)" 2½(3½, 4½)"

8 (9, 10¼)" 8 (9, 10¼)"

**RIGHT
FRONT** **LEFT
FRONT**

28" 28"

8 (9¾, 11½)" 6¼" 9 (10½, 12½)"

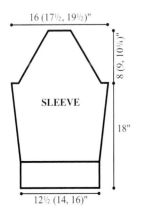

16 (17½, 19½)"

8 (9, 10¼)"

SLEEVE

18"

12½ (14, 16)"

Men's Sweaters

This collection of handknit designs for men includes practical, all-weather sweaters in rich wool tweeds, chunky stitch cables, and traditional Fair Isle patterns. Each style is a classic and right in the mainstream of current fashion.

BOUTIQUE
KNITS
FOR MEN

Photo: Palumbo

This cable classic proves that rugged good looks never go out of style—they just get better with age. The bulky Aran gets its earthy, tonal texture from the marled effect of the heather yarn. Shown in size Medium. The Chunky Cabled Pullover first appeared in the Fall 1961 issue of the original *Vogue Knitting* magazine.

Chunky Cabled Pullover

FOR INTERMEDIATE KNITTERS

SIZES
To fit Small (Medium, Large). Directions are for smallest size with larger sizes in parentheses. If there is only one figure, it applies to all sizes.

KNITTED MEASUREMENTS
● Chest 44 (48, 52)"/111.5 (122, 132)cm.
● Length 27 (27½, 28)"/68.5 (69.5, 71)cm.
● Upper arm 18½ (20, 21)"/48 (51, 53)cm.

MATERIALS
● 6 (7, 8) 8oz/250g hanks (each approx 310yds/279m) of Wool Pak Yams NZ/Baabajoes Wool Co. *14 Ply* (wool 5) in #21 heather
● One pair each sizes 11 and 13 (8 and 9mm) needles OR SIZE TO OBTAIN GAUGE
● Cable needle
● Stitch holder

GAUGE
12 sts and 13 rows to 4"/10cm over pat sts foll chart using a double strand of yarn and size 13 (9mm) needles. FOR PERFECT FIT, TAKE TIME TO CHECK GAUGE.

Notes
1 Work with a double strand of yarn throughout.

2 Due to the bulkiness of this design, the finished measurements may not correspond exactly with the schematic pieces.

STITCH GLOSSARY
Left Twist (LT)
Pass in back of first st and k 2nd st tbl, then k first st and let both sts fall from needle.
Right Twist (RT)
Pass in front of first st and k 2nd st, then k first st and let both sts fall from needle.
4-st LC
Sl 2 sts to cn and hold to *front*, k2, k2 from cn.
4-st RC
Sl 2 sts to cn and hold to *back*, k2, k2 from cn.
5-st LPC/RT
Sl 2 sts to cn and hold to *front*, p next 3 sts, work RT over 2 sts from cn.
5-st RPC/LT
Sl next 3 sts to cn and hold to *back*, LT over next 2 sts, p3 sts from cn.
5-st LPC/LT
Sl next 2 sts to cn and hold to *front*, p next 3 sts, work LT over 2 sts from cn.
5-st RPC/RT
Sl 3 sts to cn and hold to *back*, RT over next 2 sts, p3 from cn.
Bobble
Rows 9, 13 or 17 K1, p1, k1, p1, k1 loosely into space between last st worked and next st on LH needle.
Rows 10, 14 or 18 Sl 1 purlwise (see chart), p5 tog (the 5 made sts on previous row), pass the sl st over the 5 tog.

BACK
With smaller needles and a double strand of yarn, cast on 69 (75, 83) sts. Work in k1, p1 rib for 2"/5cm, inc 1 st on last (RS) row—70 (76, 84) sts. Change to larger needles.
Preparation row (WS) Foll chart from left to right (for WS rows), work sts 43 to 31 (46 to 31, 45 to 35 then 46 to 31), then work sts 30 to 1 for 30-st rep once, work sts 30 to 4 (30 to 1, 30 to 4). Cont to foll chart with pat as set up, rep rows 1-20 until piece measures 25½ (26, 26½)"/65 (66, 67)cm from beg.

Shoulder shaping
Bind off 7 (8, 9) sts at beg of next 4 rows, 8 (8, 10) sts at beg of next 2 rows. Bind off rem 26 (28, 28) sts for back neck.

FRONT
Work as for back until piece measures 25 (25½, 26)"/64 (65, 66)cm from beg.

Neck shaping
Next row (RS) Work 26 (28, 32) sts, sl center 18 (20, 20) sts to a holder, work to end. Working both sides at once, dec 1 st each neck edge *every* row 4 times, AT SAME TIME, when same length as back, shape shoulders as for back.

SLEEVES
With smaller needles and a double strand of yarn, cast on 30 sts. Work in k1, p1 rib for 3"/7.5cm. Change to larger needles.

Preparation row (RS) Foll chart from left to right (for WS rows), beg with st 23, work pat foll chart through st 1, then work sts 30 to 24 once. Cont to foll chart with pat as set up, rep rows 1-20 and inc 1 st each side in pat every other row 4 (5, 7) times, every 4th row 9 (10, 10) times—56 (60, 64) sts. Work even until piece measures 19½ (20, 20½)"/49.5 (51, 52)cm from beg. Bind off.

FINISHING

Block pieces to measurements. Sew one shoulder seam. With smaller needles and a double strand of yarn, pick up and k 58 (62, 62) sts evenly around neck edge, including sts from holder. Beg with a p row on WS, work in St st for 4 rows. Bind off. Sew other shoulder and neckband seam. Place markers at 9¼ (10, 10½)"/24 (25.5, 26.5)cm down from shoulders on front and back. Sew sleeves between markers. Sew side and sleeve seams.

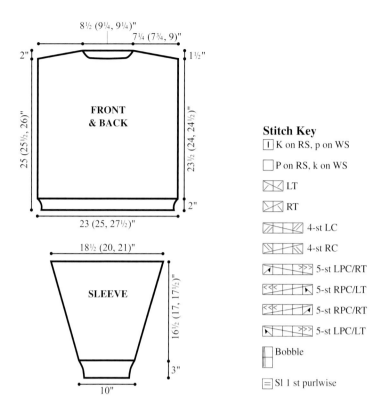

Stitch Key

- ⊥ K on RS, p on WS
- ☐ P on RS, k on WS
- ⊠ LT
- ⊠ RT
- ⊟ 4-st LC
- ⊠ 4-st RC
- 5-st LPC/RT
- 5-st RPC/LT
- 5-st RPC/RT
- 5-st LPC/LT
- ▐ Bobble
- ⊟ Sl 1 st purlwise

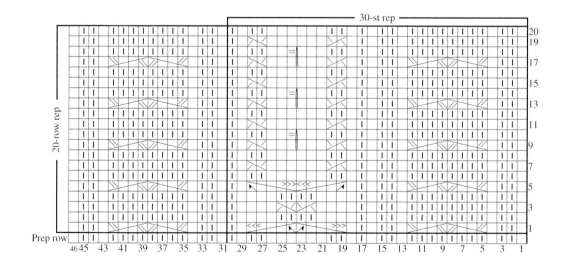

Fair Isle Pullover

This handsome Fair Isle sweater gets its fresh, hand-crafted appeal from natural, richly dyed wools. Knit in one piece, the easy-going pullover is loose-fitting with a circular yoke that decreases to a foldover crewneck. Shown in size Medium. The Fair Isle Pullover first appeared in the Fall/Winter 1957 issue of the original *Vogue Knitting* magazine.

Photo: Paul Himmel

Fair Isle Pullover

FOR EXPERIENCED KNITTERS

SIZES
To fit Small (Medium, Large). Directions are for smallest size with larger sizes in parentheses. If there is only one figure, it applies to all sizes.

KNITTED MEASUREMENTS
● Chest 44 (47, 50)"/109 (117, 124)cm.
● Length 28½ (29, 29½)"/72.5 (73.5, 75)cm.
● Upper arm 17¼ (18, 19¼)"/43 (45, 48)cm.

MATERIALS
● 10 (11, 12) 1¾oz/50g balls (each approx 99yds/90m) of Manos del Uruguay/Design Source *500 Tex* (wool 4) in #43 juniper (MC)
● 2 balls in #48 cherry (A)
● 1 ball each in #52 cameo (B), #46 malachite (C) and #08 black (D)
● Sizes 4 and 6 (3.5 and 4mm) circular needles, 36"/90cm long OR SIZE TO OBTAIN GAUGE
● Sizes 4 and 6 (3.5 and 4mm) circular needles, 16"/40cm long
● 1 set (4) dpn sizes 4 and 6 (3.5 and 4mm)
● Stitch holders and stitch markers

GAUGE
20 sts and 28 rnds to 4"/10cm over St st using size 6 (4mm) needles.

FOR PERFECT FIT, TAKE TIME TO CHECK GAUGE.

Notes
1 To simulate a circular piece, work a flat gauge swatch by k across row and breaking yarn at end of row. Reattach at beg of row. Slide sts back to beg and k across row again.
2 Sweater is knit in one piece from the neck down.
3 Read all chart rnds from right to left.
4 Carry each color, twisting yarns every 3 to 4 sts on WS across rnds.

YOKE
With smaller 16"/40cm needle and MC, beg at top of crewneck, cast on 104 (110, 114) sts. Join, taking care not to twist sts on needle. Place marker for end of rnd, and sl marker every rnd. Work in k1, p1 rib for 2"/5cm, inc 1 (0, 1) st at end of last rnd—105 (110, 115) sts. Change to larger 16"/40cm needle.
(**Note:** When there are too many sts for 16"/40cm needle, change to 36"/90cm needle.) Work in St st (k every rnd) as foll:
Next rnd [K4, inc 1 st in next st] 21 (22, 23) times—126 (132, 138) sts. Work 2 rnds even.
Next rnd [K5, inc 1 st in next st] 21 (22, 23) times—147 (154, 161) sts. Work 2 rnds even.
Next rnd [K6, inc 1 st in next st] 21 (22, 23) times—168 (176, 184) sts. K next rnd, inc 0 (4, 8) sts evenly around—168 (180, 192) sts. Work 1 rnd even.

Beg chart #1
Rnd 1 Work 12-st rep of chart 14 (15, 16) times. Cont in chart pat, working inc sts as shown on chart, until all 65 rows of chart have been worked—350 (375, 400) sts. Cut all colors except MC.

Divide for back, front and sleeves
Cont in St st with MC only as foll:
Next rnd Cast on 5 sts, k99 (107, 114) sts, place next 76 (80, 86) sts on a holder for sleeve, cast on 10 sts, k99 (108, 114) sts, place next 76 (80, 86) sts on a holder for 2nd sleeve, cast on 5 sts—218 (235, 248) sts on needle. Join. Cont in St st on these sts only for body for 12 (12½, 13)"/30 (31.5, 32.5)cm. Change to smaller 36"/90cm needle and work in k1, p1 rib for 2½"/6.5cm. Bind off loosely in rib.

SLEEVES
(**Note:** When there are too few sts to fit circular needle, change to dpn.)
With larger 16"/40cm circular needle, work across sts of sleeve as foll:
Beg in center of underarm, pick up and k 1 st in next 5 underarm cast-on sts of body, then work sleeve sts from holder to needle, then pick up last 5 underarm cast-on sts—86 (90, 96) sts. Place a marker and join. Work in St st with MC only, dec 1 st each side of marker every 4th rnd 4 (8, 16) times, every 6th rnd 9 (7, 2) times—60 sts. Work even if necessary until sleeve measures 10 (10½,

11)"/25 (26.5, 27.5)cm. Work 18 rnds of chart #2. Change to smaller dpn. Work in k1, p1 rib for 3"/7.5cm. Bind off loosely in rib.

FINISHING
Fold neckband in half to WS and sew in place.

Chart 2

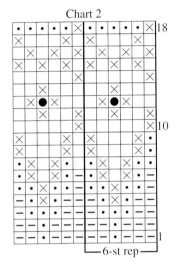

18
10
1
—6-st rep—

Color Key
- $-$ Juniper (MC)
- $\times$ Cherry (A)
- ☐ Cameo (B)
- $\cdot$ Malachite (C)
- ● Black (D)
- Γ Inc 1 st

Chart 1
25 sts

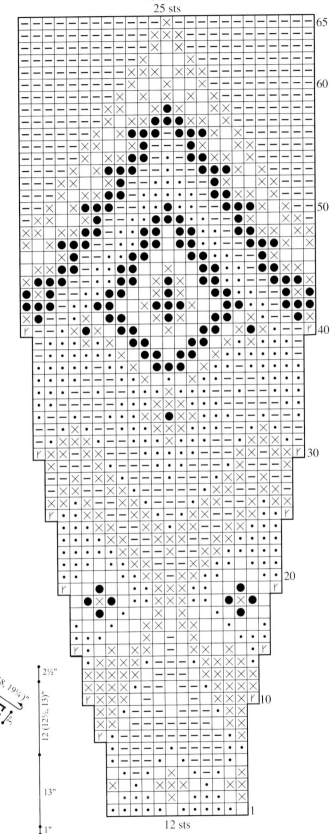

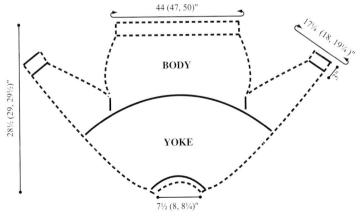

Thick rope cables, ribbings, garter stitch welts, and seed stitch panels lend to the rugged good looks of this classic crewneck. Shown in size 38. The Textured and Cabled Pullover first appeared in the Fall/Winter 1956 issue of the original *Vogue Knitting* magazine.

Textured and Cabled Pullover

FOR INTERMEDIATE KNITTERS

SIZES
To fit 36 (38, 40, 42, 44)"/91 (96, 101, 106, 112)cm chest. Directions are for smallest size with larger sizes in parentheses. If there is only one figure, it applies to all sizes.

KNITTED MEASUREMENTS
● Chest 40½ (42, 44, 46, 47½)"/103 (108, 112, 116, 121)cm.
● Length 24½ (25½, 26, 27, 27½)"/61.5 (64.5, 65.5, 67.5, 69)cm.
● Upper arm 16¾ (17¼, 17¼, 18, 19)"/42.5 (43.5, 43.5, 46, 48)cm.

MATERIALS
Original Yarn
● 15 (16, 17, 18, 19) 1¾oz/50g balls (each approx 103yds/95m) of Berroco, Inc. *Cambridge Tweed* (wool/acrylic/polyester 4) in #9374 grey/green tweed
Substitute Yarn
● 8 (9, 9, 10, 10) 3½oz/100g balls (each approx 202yds/185m) of Naturally/S.R. Kertzer, Ltd. *Tussock Double Knit 8 Ply* (wool/polyester 3) in #268 grey tweed
● One pair each sizes 5 and 7 (3.75 and 4.5mm) needles OR SIZE TO OBTAIN GAUGE
● Size 5 (3.75mm) circular needle, 16"/40cm long
● Cable needle (cn)

Note
The original yarn used for this sweater is no longer available. A comparable substitution has been made, which is available at the time of printing. Check gauge of substitute yarns very carefully before beginning.

GAUGES
● 18 sts and 28 rows to 4"/10cm over seed st using size 7 (4.5mm) needles.
● 23 sts to 3½"/9cm over cable/block pat using size 7 (4.5mm) needles.
FOR PERFECT FIT, TAKE TIME TO CHECK GAUGES.

STITCH GLOSSARY
6-st Right Cable
Sl 3 sts to cn and hold to *back*, k3, k3 from cn.
Seed Stitch
Row 1 (RS) K1, *p1, k1; rep from * to end.
Row 2 K the purl sts and p the knit sts.
Rep row 2 for seed st.

BACK
With smaller needles, cast on 110 (114, 118, 122, 126) sts. Work in k2, p2 rib for 3½"/9cm, inc 9 sts evenly across last row—119 (123, 127, 131, 135) sts. Change to larger needles.

Beg cable/block and seed st pats
Row 1 (RS) Work 5 (7, 9, 11, 13) sts in seed st, 23 sts in cable/block pat (foll chart), 9 sts in seed st, work first 22 sts of cable/block chart once, then all 23 sts

once more (45 sts total), work 9 sts in seed st, 23 sts of cable/block chart, 5 (7, 9, 11, 13) sts in seed st. Cont in this way until piece measures 14½ (15, 15½, 16, 16)"/36.5 (38, 39, 40, 40)cm from beg, end with a WS row.

Armhole shaping
Bind off 3 (4, 4, 5, 5) sts at beg of next 2 rows, then dec 1 st each side every other row 2 (3, 3, 4, 4) times—109 (109, 113, 113, 117) sts. Work even until armhole measures 9 (9½, 9½, 10, 10½)"/22.5 (24, 24, 25, 26.5)cm, end with a WS row.

Shoulder and neck shaping
Bind off 7 sts at beg of next 6 (6, 4, 4, 2) rows, 8 sts at beg of next 2 (2, 4, 4, 6) rows, AT SAME TIME, bind off center 33 (33, 35, 35, 37) sts, and working both sides at once, bind off from each neck edge 3 sts 3 times.

FRONT
Work as for back until armhole measures 7 (7½, 7½, 8, 8½)"/17.5 (19, 19, 20, 21.5)cm, end with a WS row.

Neck shaping
Next row (RS) Work 46 (46, 47, 47, 48) sts, join 2nd ball of yarn and bind off 17 (17, 19, 19, 21) sts, work to end. Working both sides at once, bind off from each neck edge 3 sts 3 times, 2 sts 3 times, then dec 1 st every other row twice, AT SAME TIME, when same length as back to shoulder, work shoulder shaping as for back.

SLEEVES

With smaller needles, cast on 42 (46, 46, 50, 50) sts. Work in k2, p2 rib for 3½"/9cm, inc 13 (11, 11, 9, 9) sts evenly across last row—55 (57, 57, 59, 59) sts. Change to larger needles.

Beg cable/block and seed st pats

Row 1 (RS) Work 5 (6, 6, 7, 7) sts in seed st, work first 22 sts of cable/block chart once, then all 23 sts once more (45 sts total), work 5 (6, 6, 7, 7) sts in seed st. Cont in this way, inc 1 st each side (working inc sts into seed st) every 6th row 12 (11, 10, 12, 18) times, every 8th row 5 (6, 7, 6, 2) times—89 (91, 91, 95, 99) sts. Work even until piece measures 20 (20½, 21, 21, 21½)"/50 (51.5, 52.5, 52.5, 54)cm from beg, end with a WS row.

Cap shaping

Bind off 3 (4, 4, 5, 5) sts at beg of next 2 rows, 2 sts at beg of next 16 (16, 16, 28, 32) rows, 3 sts at beg of next 10 (10, 10, 2, 0) rows. Bind off rem 21 (21, 21, 23, 25) sts.

FINISHING

Block pieces. Sew shoulder seams

Neckband

With RS facing and circular needle, beg at right shoulder, pick up and k116 (116, 120, 120, 124) sts evenly around neck edge. Join and work in k2, p2 rib for 1¼"/3cm. Bind off in rib. Set in sleeves. Sew side and sleeve seams.

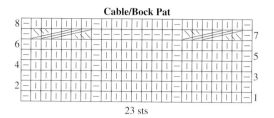

Cable/Bock Pat

23 sts

Stitch Key

☐ K on RS, p on WS

⊟ P on RS, k on WS

▱ 6-st cable

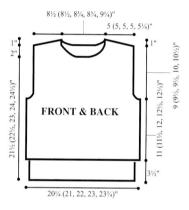

FRONT & BACK

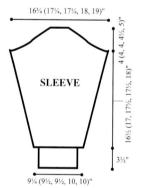

SLEEVE

Classic Cabled V-Neck

This timeless, cable classic will never go out of style. Ideal for cold weather wear, this man's V-neck pullover has been updated with looser proportions for today's relaxed look. Shown in size Medium/Large. The Classic Cabled V-Neck first appeared in the Spring/Summer 1961 issue of the original *Vogue Knitting* magazine.

Classic Cabled V-Neck

FOR INTERMEDIATE KNITTERS

SIZES
To fit X-Small/Small (Medium/ Large, X-Large). Directions are for smallest size with larger sizes in parentheses. If there is only one figure, it applies to all sizes.

KNITTED MEASUREMENTS
● Chest 42 (49, 56)"/106.5 (124, 142)cm.
● Length 26½ (27, 28)"/67 (68.5, 71)cm.
● Upper arm 17½ (19, 20)"/44.5 (48, 51)cm.

MATERIALS
● 21 (23, 26) 1¾oz/50g balls (each approx 86yds/80m) of Dale of Norway *Free Style* (wool 3) in #0020 ecru
● One pair each sizes 6 and 8 (4 and 5mm) needles OR SIZE TO OBTAIN GAUGE
● Size 6 (4mm) circular needle, 24"/60cm long
● Cable needle

GAUGE
24 sts and 26 rows to 4"/10cm over pat st foll chart using size 8 (5mm) needles. FOR PERFECT FIT, TAKE TIME TO CHECK GAUGE.

STITCH GLOSSARY
3-st RPC
Sl 1 st to cn and hold to *back*, k2, p1 from cn.

3-st LPC
Sl 2 sts to cn and hold to *front*, p1, k2 from cn.

4-st RC
Sl 2 sts to cn and hold to *back*, k2, k2 from cn.

4-st LC
Sl 2 sts to cn and hold to *front*, k2, k2 from cn.

5-st RPC
Sl 3 sts to cn and hold to *back*, k2, p3 from cn.

BACK
With smaller needles, cast on 110 (128, 144) sts. Work in k1, p1 rib for 2½"/6.5cm, inc 16 (20, 26) sts evenly spaced across last WS row—126 (148, 170) sts. Change to larger needles.

Beg chart pat
Row 1 (RS) Work sts 1 to 24, then work 22-st rep (sts 3 to 24) 4 (5, 6) times more, work sts 25 to 38. Cont in pat foll chart, rep rows 3 to 26, until piece measures 16"/40.5cm from beg.

Armhole shaping
Bind off 3 (5, 5) sts at beg of next 2 rows. Dec 1 st each side of next row then every other row 1 (4, 7) times more—116 (128, 144) sts. Work even until armhole measures 9½ (10, 11)"/24 (25.5, 28)cm.

Shoulder shaping
Bind off 12 (14, 17) sts at beg of next 4

rows 13 (15, 17) sts at beg of next 2 rows. Bind off rem 42 sts for back neck.

FRONT
Work as for back until armhole measures 2½ (3, 4)"/6.5 (7.5, 10)cm.

V-neck shaping
Next row (RS) Work 56 (62, 70) sts, k2tog, join a 2nd ball of yarn and k2tog, work to end. Cont to work both sides with separate balls of yarn, dec 1 st from each neck edge every other row 18 times more, every 4th row twice. When same length as back, bind off for shoulders as for back.

SLEEVES
With smaller needles, cast on 50 sts. Work in k1, p1 rib for 2½"/6.5cm, inc 6 sts evenly on last WS row—56 sts. Change to larger needles.

Beg chart pat
Row 1 (RS) Work sts 3 to 24 (22-st rep) twice, then work sts 25 to 36 once. Cont to foll chart in this way, inc 1 st each side (working inc sts into chart pat) every other row 9 (15, 16) times, every 4th row 16 (14, 16) times—106 (114, 120) sts. Work even until piece measures 19"/48cm from beg.

Cap shaping
Bind off 3 (5, 5) sts at beg of next 2 rows. Dec 1 st each side of next row then every other row twice more, bind

off 2 sts at beg of next 18 rows, bind off 3 sts at beg of next 6 rows—40 (44, 50) sts. Bind off.

FINISHING
Block pieces to measurements. Sew shoulder seams.

Neckband
Beg at right side of V-neck, with circular needle, pick up and k 139 sts evenly around neck edge. Do not join but working back and forth in rows, work in k1, p1 rib until band measures 1¼"/3cm. Bind off in rib. Sew neckband at center, overlapping right over left side. Sew sleeves into armholes. Sew side and sleeve seams.

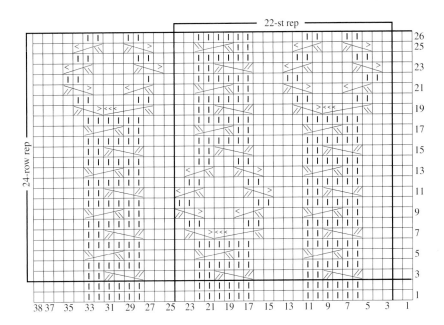

Stitch Key

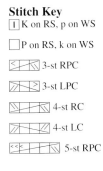

I K on RS, p on WS

P on RS, k on WS

3-st RPC

3-st LPC

4-st RC

4-st LC

5-st RPC

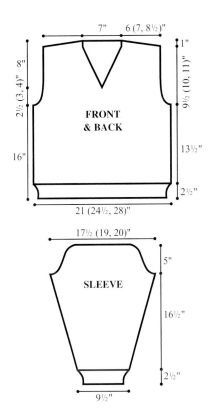

FRONT & BACK

SLEEVE

Photo: Jerrold Schatzberg

A rugged mix of an easy, mock cable stitch and deep ribbing between the cables gives this hardy pullover a manly air. The sweater features a boatneck and set-in sleeves. Shown in size 42. The Mock Cable Pullover first appeared in the Fall/Winter 1962 issue of the original *Vogue Knitting* magazine.

Mock Cable Pullover

FOR INTERMEDIATE KNITTERS

SIZES
To fit 38 (40, 42, 44)"/96 (101, 106, 112)cm chest. Directions are for smallest size with larger sizes in parentheses. If there is only one set of figures, it applies to all sizes.

KNITTED MEASUREMENTS
● Chest 41 (43, 45, 47)"/102 (108, 112, 118)cm.
● Length 25½ (26, 26, 26½)"/65 (66, 66, 67.5)cm.
● Upper arm 15½ (16½, 16½, 17)"/39 (41, 41, 42.5)cm.

MATERIALS
Original Yarn
● 10 (11, 11, 12) 3½oz/100g balls (each approx 77yds/70m) of Phildar *Reine Schafwolle* (wool 6) in #729 red
Substitute Yarn
● 7 (7, 7, 8) 4oz/113g balls (each approx 125yds/114m) of Brown Sheep Co. *Lamb's Pride Bulky* (wool 4) in #M180 red
● One pair size 13 (9mm) needles OR SIZE TO OBTAIN GAUGE

Note
The original yarn used for this sweater is no longer available. A comparable substitution has been made, which is available at the time of printing. Check gauge of substitute yarns very carefully before beginning.

GAUGE
9 sts and 12 rows to 3"/7.5cm over pat st using size 13 (9mm) needles. FOR PERFECT FIT, TAKE TIME TO CHECK GAUGE.

STITCH GLOSSARY
Pattern Stitch
Row 1 (RS) *P2, k3, p2, k next st into row below; rep from * to end.
Row 2 *P1, k2, p3, k2; rep from * to end.
Row 3 Rep row 1.
Row 4 *P1, k2, k3tog loosely but do not drop sts from LH needle, p same 3 sts tog, then k same 3 sts tog, drop sts from LH needle (mock cable made over 3 sts), k2; rep from * to end. Rep rows 1-4 for pat st.

BACK
Cast on 49 (51, 53, 55) sts. Work in k1, p1 rib for 1½"/4cm, inc 12 (14, 14, 16) sts evenly across last row—61 (65, 67, 71) sts.

Beg pat st
For sizes 38 and 44 only—Row 1 (RS)
P1 (2), k3, p2, k next st into row below; rep from * of row 1 of pat st, end last rep p1 (2).
Row 2 K1 (2), p3, k2; rep from * of row 2 of pat st, end last rep k1 (2).
Row 3 Rep row 1.
Row 4 K1 (2), work mock cable over next 3 sts, k2; rep from * of row 4 of pat st, end last rep k1 (2). Rep rows 1-4 for pat st.

For sizes 40 and 42 only—Row 1 (RS)
P0 (1), k next st into row below; rep from * of row 1 of pat st, end last rep p0 (1).
Row 2 K0 (1); rep from * of row 2 of pat st, end last rep p1, k0 (1).
Row 3 Rep row 1.
Row 4 K0 (1); rep from * of row 4 of pat st, end last rep p1, k0 (1). Rep rows 1-4 for pat st.

For all sizes: Cont in pat as established until piece measures 16½"/42cm from beg, or desired length to underarm, end with a WS row.

Armhole shaping
Keeping to pat, bind off 3 sts at beg of next 2 rows. Dec 1 st each side every other row 5 times—45 (49, 51, 55) sts. Work even in pat until armhole measures 9 (9½, 9½, 10)"/23 (24, 24, 25.5)cm, end with a WS row.
Next row (RS) Work in k1, p1 rib, and dec 10 sts evenly across—35 (39, 41, 45) sts. Work in k1, p1 rib for 1½"/4cm. Bind off in rib.

FRONT
Work as for back.

SLEEVES
Cast on 25 (27, 27, 29) sts. Work in k1, p1 rib for 3½"/9cm, inc 8 sts evenly spaced across last WS row—33 (35, 35, 37) sts.

Beg pat st
Row 1 (RS) P0 (1, 1, 2), k next st into row below; rep from * of row 1 of pat st,

end p0 (1, 1, 2). Cont in pat as established, inc 1 st each side every 6th row 3 (2, 2, 1) times, then every 8th row 4 (5, 5, 6) times—47 (49, 49, 51) sts. Work even in pat until piece measures 18 (18½, 18½, 19)"/45.5 (47, 47, 48)cm from beg, or desired length to underarm, end with a WS row.

Cap shaping

Bind off 3 sts at beg of next 2 rows. Dec 1 st each side every other row 8 (9, 9, 10) times—25 sts. Bind off 3 sts at beg of next 4 rows. Bind off rem 13 sts.

FINISHING

Block pieces to measurements. Overlap rib at top of front and back and sew shoulder seams through both thicknesses, leaving center 10"/25.5cm open for neck. Sew side and sleeve seams. Set in sleeves.

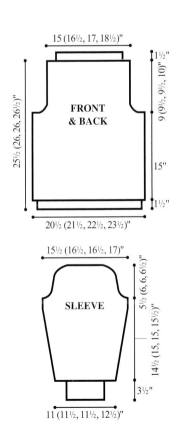

15 (16½, 17, 18½)"

1½"

9 (9½, 9½, 10)"

FRONT & BACK

25½ (26, 26, 26½)"

15"

1½"

20½ (21½, 22½, 23½)"

15½ (16½, 16½, 17)"

5½ (6, 6, 6½)"

SLEEVE

14½ (15, 15, 15½)"

3½"

11 (11½, 11½, 12½)"

Babies and Children

Knitwear for the well-dressed child...this chapter offers a nostalgic look at babies' and children's wear, from cozy cover-ups knit in soft yarns, to playful rompers, pullovers, and cardigans—there's even a sparkling party dress for fancy occasions.

Here's a good-looking sweater for your little tough guy. This handsome striped turtleneck is ready for anything, from the hardest wear to the roughest weather. The Boy's Striped Turtleneck first appeared in the special Kids' 1966 issue of the original *Vogue Knitting* magazine.

Boy's Striped Turtleneck

VERY EASY VERY VOGUE

SIZES
To fit child's size 4 (6, 8). Directions are for smallest size with larger sizes in parentheses. If there is only one figure, it applies to all sizes.

KNITTED MEASUREMENTS
● Chest 27 (30, 33)"/68.5 (76, 83.5)cm.
● Length 17 (18, 19)"/43 (45.5, 48)cm.
● Upperarm 10 (11, 12)"/25.5 (28, 30.5)cm.

MATERIALS
● 3 (4, 5) 1¾oz/50g balls (each approx 100yds/91m) of Brown Sheep *Lambs Pride Superwash* (wool 4) each in #SW71 blue (A) and #SW37 brown (B)
● One pair each sizes 7 and 8 (4.5 and 5mm) needles OR SIZE TO OBTAIN GAUGE
● Size 7 (4.5mm) circular needle, 16"/40cm long
● Stitch holders

GAUGE
19 sts and 24 rows to 4"/10cm over St st using size 8 (5mm) needles. FOR PERFECT FIT, TAKE TIME TO CHECK GAUGE.

STITCH GLOSSARY
Stripe Pattern
4 rows B, 6 rows A, 6 rows B, 6 rows A, 8 rows B, 6 rows A, 2 rows B.

BACK
With smaller needles and A, cast on 64 (72, 78) sts. Work in k1, p1 rib for 1½"/4cm. Change to larger needles and work in St st until piece measures 4½ (5, 5½)"/11.5 (12.5, 14)cm from beg. Work 38 rows stripe pat—piece measures approx 11 (11½, 12)"/28 (29, 30.5)cm from beg. Cont with B to end of piece.

Armhole shaping
Bind off 3 sts at beg of next 2 rows. Dec 1 st each side every other row 1 (3, 5) times—56 (60, 62) sts. Work even until armhole measures 5 (5½, 6)"/12.5 (14, 15.5)cm.

Shoulder and neck shaping
Bind off 6 sts at beg of next 4 (2, 2) rows, 7 sts at beg of next 2 (4, 4) rows. Bind off rem 18 (20, 22) sts for back neck.

FRONT
Work as for back until piece measures 14½ (15½, 16½)"/36.5 (39, 41.5)cm from beg, end with a WS row.

Shoulder and neck shaping
Next row (RS) K 22 (23, 23), place center 12 (14, 16) sts on a holder, join a 2nd ball of yarn and k to end. Working both sides at once, dec 1 st at each neck edge every other row 3 times—19 (20, 20) each side. Work even until same length as back to

shoulders. Shape shoulders as for back.

SLEEVES
With smaller needles and A, cast on 36 (38, 38) sts. Work in k1, p1 rib for 1½"/4cm. Change to larger needles and work in St st until piece measures 4½ (5½, 6½)"/11.5 (14, 16.5)cm from beg, then work in stripe pat, AT SAME TIME, inc 1 st each side every 8th (8th, 6th) 6 (7, 10) times—48 (52, 58) sts. Work even until all 38 stripe rows have been worked—piece measures approx 11 (12, 13)"/28 (30.5, 33)cm from beg. Cont with B to end of piece.

Cap shaping
Bind off 3 sts at beg of next 2 rows, 2 sts at beg of next 4 (6, 6) rows. Dec 1 st each side every other row 4 (4, 6) times. Bind off 3 sts at beg of next 2 rows, 4 sts at beg of next 2 rows. Bind off rem 12 (12, 14) sts.

FINISHING
Block pieces to measurement. Sew shoulder seams.

Turtleneck
With RS facing, circular needle and B, pick up and k 60 (64, 68) sts evenly around neck. Join and work in rnds of k1, p1 rib for 4"/10cm. Change to A and p 1 row. Cont in rib and A for 1"/2.5cm more. Bind off loosely in rib. Set in sleeves. Sew side and sleeve seams.

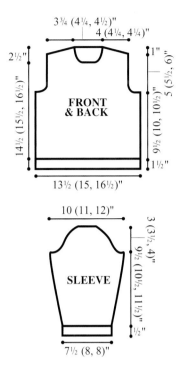

3¾ (4¼, 4½)"
4 (4¼, 4¼)"

2½ "

1"

5 (5½, 6)"

9½ (10, 10½)"

FRONT & BACK

14½ (15½, 16½)"

1½"

13½ (15, 16½)"

10 (11, 12)"

3 (3½, 4)"

9½ (10½, 11½)"

SLEEVE

½"

7½ (8, 8)"

What girl wouldn't love this easy-wear, zip-front cardigan classic with a fluffy tassel closure. Red and white striped borders accent this summer navy sweater. The Girl's Zip-Front Cardigan first appeared in the special Kids' 1966 issue of the original *Vogue Knitting* magazine.

Girl's Zip-Front Cardigan

FOR INTERMEDIATE KNITTERS

SIZES

To fit child's size 4 (6, 8). Directions are for smallest size with larger sizes in parentheses. If there is only one figure, it applies to all sizes.

KNITTED MEASUREMENTS

● Chest 26 (28, 30)"/66 (71, 76)cm.
● Length 16 (16½, 18)"/40.5 (42, 45.5)cm.
● Upperarm 9½ (10¼, 11)"/24 (26, 28)cm.

MATERIALS

● 7 (7, 8) 1¾oz/50g balls (each approx 123yds/113m) of Rowan Yarns *Wool Cotton* (wool/cotton 3) in #909 navy (MC)
● 1 ball each in # 900 ecru (A) and #911 red (B)
● One pair size 8 (5mm) needles OR SIZE TO OBTAIN GAUGE
● Size 8 (5mm) circular needle, 32"/80cm long
● One separating zipper 14 (14, 16)"/35 (35, 40)cm long
● Stitch holder

GAUGE

24 sts and 32 rows to 4"/10cm over garter st using size 8 (5mm) needles. FOR PERFECT FIT, TAKE TIME TO CHECK GAUGE.

BACK

With A, cast on 78 (84, 90) sts. Working in garter st, work border as foll: 2 rows A, 2 rows B, 2 rows A. Change to MC and cont in garter st until piece measures 10¼ (10¼, 11¼)"/ 26 (26, 28.5)cm from beg.

Armhole shaping

Bind off 3 sts at beg of next 2 rows. Dec 1 st each side every other row 1 (2, 3) times—70 (74, 78) sts. Work even until armhole measures 5 (5½, 6)"/12.5 (14, 15)cm.

Shoulder shaping

Bind off 6 sts at beg of next 4 rows, 7 (8, 9) sts at beg of next 2 rows. Place rem 32 (34, 36) sts on a holder for back neck.

LEFT FRONT

With A, cast on 39 (43, 45) sts. K 1 row.
Next row (WS) K2tog, k to end. Change to B and k 1 row.
Next row K2tog, k to end. Change to A and k 1 row.
Next row K2tog, k to end—36 (40, 42) sts. Change to MC and cont in garter st until same length as back to armhole. Shape armhole at side edge (beg of RS rows) as for back—32 (35, 36) sts. Work even until piece measures 14 (14, 16)"/35 (35, 40)cm from beg, end with a RS row.

Neck and shoulder shaping

Next row (WS) Bind off 7 (9, 9) sts (neck edge), work to end. Cont to bind off from neck edge 2 sts once, dec 1 st every other row 4 times, AT SAME TIME, when same length as back to shoulder, shape shoulder at side edge as for back.

RIGHT FRONT

Work as for left front, reversing all shaping.

SLEEVES

With A, cast on 42 (46, 50) sts. Work 6 rows border as for back. Change to MC and cont in garter st as foll: work even until piece measures 2"/5cm from beg. Inc 1 st each side on next row, then every 8th row 7 times more—58 (62, 66) sts. Work even until piece measures 10½ (11½, 12½)"/26.5 (29, 31.5)cm from beg.

Cap shaping

Bind off 3 sts at beg of next 2 rows. Dec 1 st each side every other row 12 (13, 14) times. Bind off 2 sts at beg of next 6 rows. Bind off rem 16 (18, 20) sts.

FINISHING

Block pieces to measurements. Sew shoulder seams. Set in sleeves. Sew side and sleeve seams.

Neckband and border

With RS facing, circular needle and A, beg at lower right front edge above border, pick up and k 228 (246, 258) sts along right front edge, neck edge (including sts on holder), and along left front edge to border.

Row 1 Inc 1 st in first st, k to last st, inc 1.
Row 2 Change to B and k 1 row.
Row 3 With B, rep row 1.
Row 4 With A, knit.
Row 5 With A, rep row 1. Bind off loosely. Join corners at lower front edges. Sew in zipper. Make 1 large pompom with all three colors and attach to zipper pull as shown in photo.

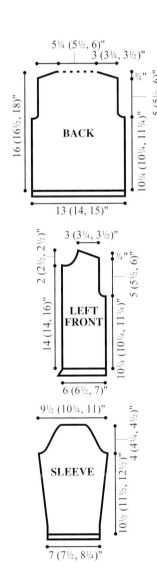

5¼ (5½, 6)"
3 (3¼, 3½)"
¾"
16 (16½, 18)"
5 (5½, 6)"
BACK
10¼ (10¼, 11¼)"
13 (14, 15)"

3 (3¼, 3½)"
2 (2½, 2½)"
¾"
14 (14, 16)"
5 (5½, 6)"
LEFT FRONT
10¼ (10¼, 11¼)"
6 (6½, 7)"

9½ (10¼, 11)"
4 (4¼, 4½)"
SLEEVE
10½ (11½, 12½)"
7 (7½, 8¼)"

Photo: Fred Baker

Make a splash! This jaunty jumper is just the thing for your little one to romp around in. Knit in a lightweight cotton, it's cool and comfy for seaside wear. The Sailboat Sun-Suit first appeared in the Spring/Summer 1954 issue of the original *Vogue Knitting* magazine.

Sailboat Sun-Suit

FOR INTERMEDIATE KNITTERS

SIZES
To fit child's size 2 (4, 6). Directions are for smallest size with larger sizes in parentheses. If there is only one figure, it applies to all sizes.

KNITTED MEASUREMENTS
● Width around leg 9½ (10, 11)"/24 (25.5, 28)cm.
● Length approx 15½ (17, 19)"/39.5 (43, 48)cm.

MATERIALS
● 3 (3, 4) 1¾oz/50g balls (each approx 167yds/155m) of Lang/Berroco *Baby Cotton* (cotton 2) in #2361 red (MC)
● 1 ball in #2301 white (CC)
● One pair each sizes 1 and 3 (2.25 and 3mm) needles OR SIZE TO OBTAIN GAUGE
● Two ¾"/20mm buttons

GAUGE
28 sts and 40 rows to 4"/10cm over St st using size 3 (3mm) needles. FOR PERFECT FIT, TAKE TIME TO CHECK GAUGE.

BACK
With larger needles and MC, beg at crotch, cast on 19 (21, 23) sts. Work in St st as foll: work 4 rows even. Cast on 2 (4, 6) sts at beg of next 2 rows, 4 sts at beg of next 16 rows—87 (93, 99)

sts. Work even until piece measures 4¼"/10.5cm from beg. Dec 1 st each side on next row, then every 7th row 3 (4, 5) times more—79 (83, 87) sts. Work even until piece measures 8 (9, 10)"/20.5 (23, 25.5)cm from beg, end with a WS row.

Back shaping
Work in short row as foll: K to last 9 sts, turn. Sl 1, p to the last 9 sts, turn. Sl 1, k to the last 18 sts, turn. Sl 1, p to the last 18 sts, turn. Sl 1, k to the last 27 sts, turn. Sl 1, p to the last 27 sts, turn. Sl 1, k across all sts. Change to smaller needles and work in k1, p1 rib for 1"/2.5cm. Bind off in rib.

FRONT
Work as for back until piece measures 8 (9, 10)"/20.5 (23, 25.5)cm from beg, end with a RS row. Change to smaller needles and work in k1, p1 rib for 1"/2.5cm,

inc 1 st on last WS row—80 (84, 88) sts. Change to larger needles

Bib
Cont in St st, bind off 15 (16, 17) sts at beg of next 2 rows—50 (52, 54) sts.
Next row (RS) Beg with k1 (p1, k1) work in k1, p1 rib over 10 (11,12) sts, work center 30 sts in St st, beg with p1, rib last 10 (11, 12) sts. Cont in pats as established for 7 (9, 11) rows more. Work 20 rows of chart pat over center 30 sts. Cont working center 30 sts in St st with MC only and rem sts in rib as established, until bib measures 3½ (4, 4½)"/9 (10, 11.5)cm from last bound-off row. Change to smaller needles and work in k1, p1 rib over all sts for 1"/2.5cm more.

Straps
Next row Rib 10 (11, 12) sts, join 2nd ball of yarn and bind off 30 sts, rib to end.

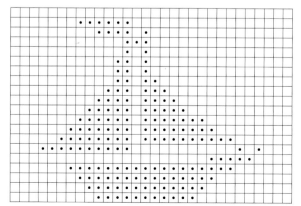

Color Key

☐ MC

⊡ CC

Working both sides at once, work even for 9½ (10½, 11½)"/24 (26.5, 29)cm more.
Next (buttonhole) row Rib 3 (3, 4) sts, bind off next 4 sts, rib to end. On next row, cast on 4 sts over bound-off sts. Work even until straps measure 10¾ (11¾, 12¾)"/27 (30, 32)cm, or desired length. Bind off in rib.

FINISHING
Block piece to measurement. Sew side seams.

Leg bands
With RS facing and smaller needles and MC, pick up 80 (84, 88) sts evenly around each leg edge. Work in k1, p1 rib for 1"/2.5cm. Bind off loosely in rib. Sew crotch and leg band seams. Sew on buttons in center of back ribbed waistband.

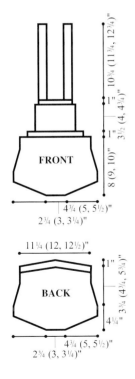

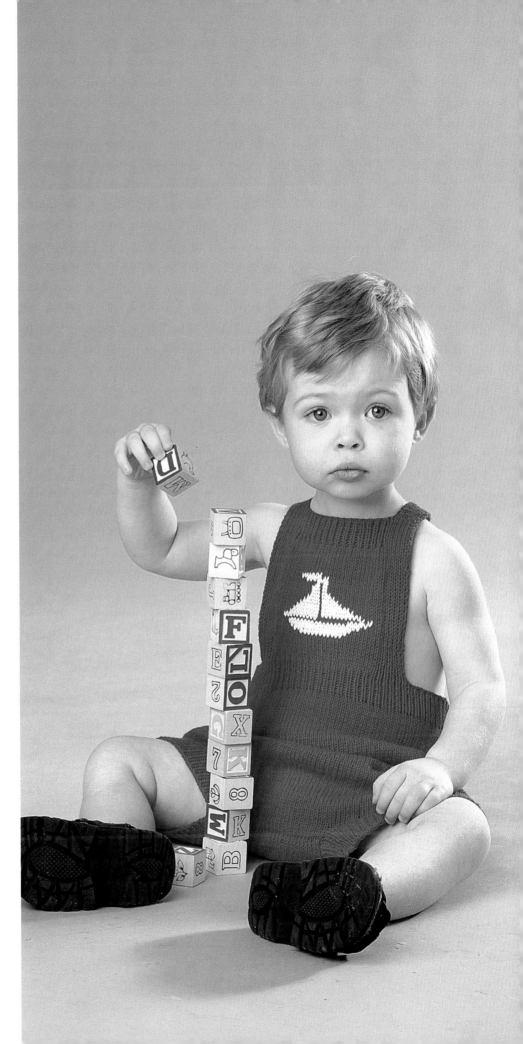

Extra-special essentials for baby in delicate white with pretty embroidered flowers and satin ribbon ties. The four-piece baby set includes a cardigan, mittens, bonnet, and booties. The Embroidered Baby Set first appeared in the Spring/Summer 1950 issue of the original *Vogue Knitting* magazine.

Embroidered Baby Set

FOR INTERMEDIATE KNITTERS

SIZES
To fit 6 months.

KNITTED MEASUREMENTS
CARDIGAN
● Chest (closed) 21½"/54.5cm.
● Length 10"/25.5cm.
● Upperarm 8"/20.5cm.

MATERIALS
● 3 1¾oz/50g balls (each approx 262yds/240m) of Patons® *Kroy 3-Ply* (wool/nylon 1) in #361 off-white (MC)
● 1 ball each in #331 yellow (A) and #333 green (B)
● One pair size 3 (3mm) needles OR SIZE TO OBTAIN GAUGE
● Size D/3 (3mm) crochet hook
● 3½yds/3.5m of ½"/13mm-wide satin ribbon

GAUGE
32 sts and 40 rows to 4"/10cm over St st using size 3 (3mm) needles.
FOR PERFECT FIT, TAKE TIME TO CHECK GAUGE.

STITCH GLOSSARY
Seed Stitch
Row 1 (RS) *K1, p1; rep from * to end.
Row 2 K the purl sts and p the knit sts.
Rep row 2 for seed st.

CARDIGAN

BACK
With MC, cast on 80 sts. Work in seed st for 1"/2.5cm. Work in St st for 1"/2.5cm, end with a WS row.
Next row (RS) K6, yo, k2tog, [k20, yo, k2tog] 3 times, k6. Cont in St st until piece measures 4½"/11.5cm from beg, end with a WS row.
Next row (RS) K17, yo, k2tog, [k20, yo, k2tog] twice, k17. Cont in St st until piece measures 6"/15cm from beg, end with a WS row.

Armhole shaping
Bind off 4 sts at beg of next 2 rows, 2 sts at beg of next 2 rows—68 sts.
Next row (RS) K2tog, [k20, yo, k2tog] twice, k20, k2tog—66 sts. Work even until piece measure 9"/23cm from beg, end with a WS row.

Neck shaping
Next row (RS) K10, yo, k2tog, k10, join 2nd ball of yarn and bind off center 22 sts, k10, yo, k2tog, k10. Work both sides at once until piece measures 10"/25.5cm from beg. Bind off 22 sts each side for shouders.

LEFT FRONT
Cast on 46 sts. Work in seed st for 1"/2.5cm, end with a WS row.
Next row (RS) Work in St st to last 6 sts, work last 6 sts in seed st for front band. Cont in pats as established until piece measures 2"/5cm from beg, end with a WS row.

Next row (RS) K8, yo, k2tog, k20, yo, k2tog, k8, work to end. Work even until piece measures 4¼"/10.5cm from beg, end with a WS row.
Next row (RS) K18, yo, k2tog, k20, work to end. Work even until piece measures 6"/15cm from beg, end with a WS row.

Armhole shaping
Bind off 4 sts at beg of next row, then 2 sts at beg of next RS row. P 1 row.
Next row (RS) K2tog, k21, yo, k2tog, k9, work to end—39 sts. Work even until piece measures 8½"/21.5cm from beg, end with a WS row.
Next row (RS) K10, yo, k2tog, work to end.

Neck shaping
Next row (WS) Bind off 17 sts, work to end. Work even until piece measures 10"/25.5cm from beg. Bind off rem 22 sts.

RIGHT FRONT
Work to correspond to left front, reversing all shaping.

SLEEVES
With MC, cast on 50 sts. Work in seed st for 1"/2.5cm. Work even in St st until piece measures 2"/5cm from beg, end with a RS row.
Next row (WS) Inc 1 st each side of row—52 sts.
Next row K14, yo, k2tog, k20, yo, k2tog, k14. Cont in pat as established, working yo rows as for back, AT SAME TIME, inc

1 st each side every 8th row 6 times more—64 sts. Work even until piece measures 7½"/19cm from beg.

Cap shaping
Bind off 3 sts at beg of next 10 rows. Bind off rem 34 sts.

FINISHING
Block pieces to measurements. Sew shoulder seams. Set in sleeves. Sew side and sleeve seams. Work RS facing, crochet hook and B, work 1 row sc evenly around neck edge, then work 1 row sc with A. With B, work 5 lazy daisy sts around first yo of first pat row on back; with A, work around 2nd yo. Make 5 lazy daisy sts in each yo, alternating colors. Cut two 14"/35.5cm lengths of ribbon and attach to each front at neck for ties (see photo).

BONNET

With MC, beg at lower back edge, cast on 32 sts. Work in seed st for 4½"/11.5 cm. Place sts on a holder. With RS facing and MC, pick up and k 33 sts along side edge of seed st panel, place 32 sts from holder onto needle, pick up 33 sts along other side edge— 98 sts. Work in St st for 1"/2.5cm, end with a WS row.

Next row (RS) K15, yo, k2tog, [k20, yo, k2tog] 3 times, k15. Cont in pat as for cardigan until piece measures 4½"/11.5cm from beg of St st. Cont in seed st for 1"/2.5cm. Bind off.

FINISHING
Turn back last 1"/2.5cm of seed st for cuff and sew in place. With RS facing, crochet hook and B, work 1 row sc evenly along back edge, then 1 row sc

with A. Cut one 30"/76cm length of ribbon and sew under cuff, leaving extra lengths on each side of cap for ties. Embroider lazy daisy sts over eyelets as for cardigan.

BOOTIES

Cast on 36 sts and work in seed st for ½"/1.5cm. Change to St st and work even for 1"/2.5cm, end with a WS row.
Next row K6, yo, k2tog, k20, yo, k2tog, k6. Cont in St st until piece measures 2¼"/5.5cm from beg. Change to seed st and work for ¼"/.5cm more.
Next (eyelet) row *K1, yo, k2tog; rep from * to end. Cont in seed st for ½"/1.5cm more.

Instep
Cont in seed st, work 26 sts, turn and work 16 sts. Work even on these 16 sts for 1¼"/3cm.
Next row Work 7 sts, yo, k2tog, work 7 sts. Cont in seed st until instep measures 2½"/6.5cm.

Foot
Cont in seed st, work 16 sts, pick up and work 16 sts along side edge of instep, work next 10 sts, turn.
Next row Work across 42 sts, pick up and work 16 sts along side edge of instep, work across rem 10 sts—68 sts. Work even for 4 rows.

Toe shaping
Work across 26 sts, place marker, k2tog, work next 12 sts, k2tog, place marker, work across rem 26 sts.
Next row K2tog, work across to marker, sl marker, k2tog, work to 2 sts before next marker, k2tog, work to last 2 sts, k2tog.

Next row Work in seed st. Rep last 2 rows 4 times more. Bind off.

FINISHING
Sew back seam. Cut two 18"/45.5cm lengths of ribbon. Run through eyelet row. Embroider as for cardigan.

MITTENS

Beg at cuff, cast on 48 sts. Work in seed st for ½"/1.5cm. Work in St st until piece measures 1½"/4cm from beg, end with a WS row.
Next row (RS) K4, yo, k2tog, [k17, yo, k2tog] twice, k4. Work in St st until piece measures 2"/5cm from beg, end with a WS row. Work in seed st for 4 rows, dec 24 sts evenly spaced across first row—24 sts.
Next (eyelet) row *K2, yo, k2tog; rep from * to end.
Next row Work in seed st, inc 8 st evenly spaced across—32 sts. Work even in seed st for 3 rows.
Next row Work in seed st, inc 8 sts evenly spaced across—40 sts. Work in seed st until 2"/5cm from last St st row of cuff.
Next row Work seed st on 10 sts, yo, k2tog, work seed st to end. Work even for 2½"/6.5cm from eyelet row. Dec 4 sts evenly spaced across next row, then every other row 3 times more—24 sts.
Next row Work in seed st, dec 8 sts evenly spaced across—16 sts.
Next row *K1, k3tog; rep from * to end. Cut yarn and draw through rem sts. Fasten off.

FINISHING
Embroider as for cardigan. Cut rem ribbon in half. Draw through eyelet row on each mitten.

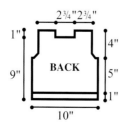

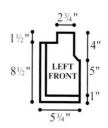

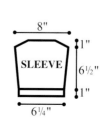

Girl's Paillette Dress

Simply dazzling! This pretty party dress with knit-in paillettes has a festive flair perfect for any dress-up occasion. Shown in size 12. The Girl's Paillette Dress first appeared in the Fall/Winter 1968 issue of the original *Vogue Knitting* magazine.

Girl's Paillette Dress

FOR EXPERIENCED KNITTERS

SIZES
Sized for child's 12 (14).

KNITTED MEASUREMENTS
- Bust 30 (32)"/76 (81)cm.
- Length 27 (28½)"/68.5 (72.5)cm.
- Upper arm 10¼ (10¾)"/26 (27)cm.

MATERIALS
- 16 (18) 1¾oz/50g balls (each approx 121yds/109m) of Skacel Collection *Prince* (tactel 4) in #600 black
- Size 8 (5mm) circular needle, 24"/60cm long OR SIZE TO OBTAIN GAUGE
- One pair size 8 (5mm) needles
- 1000 1"/2.5cm black paillettes
- Stitch holders

GAUGE
16 sts and 24 rnds to 4"/10cm over St st with paillettes using a double strand of yarn and size 8 (5mm) needles.
FOR PERFECT FIT, TAKE TIME TO CHECK GAUGE.

STITCH GLOSSARY
Stockinette Stitch with Paillettes
(worked circular on a multiple of 4 sts)
Rnds 1-5 Knit.
Rnd 6 (paillette rnd) *K3, hold a paillette in front of work, insert RH needle through paillette hole and into next st, k this st and paillette tog; rep from * around. Rep rnds 1-6 for St st with paillettes.

Notes
1 Be careful to separate paillettes as they tend to stick together.
2 Work with 2 strands of yarn held tog throughout.
3 When working back and forth in rows, paillettes can be worked on WS rows by holding paillette in back of work (to RS) and inserting RH needle into paillette hole and into next st, then p this st and paillette.

BODY
With 2 strands of yarn held tog and circular needle, cast on 120 (128) sts. Join to work in rnds. Pm to mark beg of rnd. P 1 rnd, k 1 rnd, p 1 rnd. K 4 rnds.
Next rnd Work paillette rnd 6. [K 1 rnd, p 1 rnd] twice. Then work in St st with paillettes (rnds 1-6) until piece measures 21 (22)"/53 (56)cm from beg, end with pat rnd 2.
Next rnd *Bind off 3 sts, work until there are 57 (61) sts on needle; rep from * once.

BACK
Turn and p57 (61) sts for back. Then cont on these sts only in rows as foll:
Next (dec) row (RS) K1, ssk, work pat to last 3 sts, k2tog, k1. Rep dec row every other row 5 (7) times more, end with a p row. Place 45 sts on a holder.

FRONT
Rejoin yarn to rem sts and beg with a p row, work as for back. Place 45 sts on a holder.

SLEEVES
With straight needles and 2 strands of yarn held tog, cast on 37 sts. Work back and forth in rows.
Row 1 (WS) Knit. P 1 row. K 1 row. Work 4 rows in St st.
Next (paillette) row (WS) P4, work paillette in next st, *p3, work paillette in next st; rep from *, end p4.
Next row Knit. K4 rows (for garter st). Work in St st with paillettes (in rows), inc 1 st each side every 18th row 2 (3) times—41 (43) sts. Work even until piece measures 11 (12)"/28 (30.5)cm from beg.

Raglan shaping
Bind off 2 sts at beg of next 2 rows.
Next row (RS) K1, ssk, work to last 3 sts, k2tog, k1. Rep dec row every other row 5 times more, every 4th row 0 (1) time. Work 0 (2) rows even. Place 25 sts on holder.

YOKE
With RS facing 2 strands of yarn and circular needle, work 25 sts of one sleeve 45 sts of back, 25 sts of other sleeve and 45 sts of front—140 sts. Join and pm to mark beg of rnd, (rnd worked is rnd 2). Work rnds 3-6 once, then rnds 1-6 once. K 1 rnd.
Next (dec) rnd *P5, p2tog; rep from * to end—120 sts. K 1 rnd. P 1 rnd. K 3 rnds.
Next (dec) rnd *K4, k2tog; rep from * to end—100 sts.
Next rnd *K3, work paillette in next st; rep

from * to end. [K 1 rnd, p 1 rnd] twice.
Next (dec) rnd *K3, k2tog; rep from * to
end—80 sts. P 1 rnd, k 1 rnd, p 1 rnd.
Bind off knitwise.

FINISHING
Sew sleeve seams. Sew raglan sleeve
seams.

Photo: Francesco Scavullo

A pretty sweater set with heartfelt style! Show your little girl how much you love her with this charming and soft springtime favorite. The Girl's Heart Twinset first appeared in the Spring/Summer 1959 issue of the original Vogue Knitting magazine.

Girl's Heart Twinset

FOR INTERMEDIATE KNITTERS

SIZES

To fit child's size 2 (4, 6). Directions are for smallest size with larger sizes in parentheses. If there is only one figure, it applies to all sizes.

KNITTED MEASUREMENTS

PULLOVER:
- Chest 23 (24½, 26)"/58.5 (62, 66)cm.
- Length 13½ (14½, 15½)"/ 34.5 (37, 39.5)cm.
- Upper arm 8 (8½, 9)"/20.5 (21.5, 23)cm.

CARDIGAN:
- Chest 27 (29, 31)"/68.5 (73.5, 78.5)cm.
- Length 14 (15, 16)"/35.5 (38.5, 41)cm.
- Upper arm 9 (9½, 10)"/23 (24, 25.5)cm.

MATERIALS

- 4 (5, 5) 1¾oz/50g balls (each approx 262yds/240m) of Patons *Kroy* (wool 1) in #361 white (MC)
- 1 ball in #337 red (CC)
- One pair each sizes 2 and 3 (2.5 and 3mm) needles OR SIZE TO OBTAIN GAUGE
- Size C/2 (2.5mm) crochet hook
- Two ⅜"/10mm buttons for pullover
- Eight ⅜"/10mm buttons for cardigan
- Stitch holders

GAUGE

32 sts and 38 rows to 4"/10cm over St st using size 3 (3mm) needles.
FOR PERFECT FIT, TAKE TIME TO CHECK GAUGE.

PULLOVER

FRONT

With smaller needles and MC, cast on 92 (98, 104) sts. Work in k1, p1 rib for 1½"/4cm. Change to larger needles and work in St st until piece measures 6½ (7, 7½)"/16.5 (17.7, 19)cm from beg, inc 1 st at end of last WS row—93 (99, 105) sts. Work 2 rows CC and 2 rows MC.

Beg chart

Next row (RS) Work 0 (3, 6) sts MC, work 20 st chart rep 4 times, work first 13 sts of chart once more, work 0 (3, 6) sts MC. Cont in pat as established until 12 rows of chart have been worked. Work 2 rows MC, and 2 rows CC, dec 1 st at end of last row —92 (98, 104) sts. Piece measures approx measures 8½ (9, 9½)"/21.5 (23, 24)cm from beg. Change to MC and work as foll:

Armhole shaping

Bind off 6 (6, 7) sts at beg of next 2 rows. Dec 1 st each side every other row 3 times—74 (80, 84) sts. Work even until piece measures 11½

(12½, 13½)"/29.5 (32, 34.5)cm from beg, end with a WS row.

Neck and shoulder shaping

Next row (RS) Work 28 (30, 31) sts, join 2nd ball of yarn and bind off center 18 (20, 22) sts, work to end. Working both sides at once, dec 1 st at each neck edge every other row 6 times, AT SAME TIME, when armhole measures 4½ (5, 5½)"/11.5 (12.5, 14)cm, shape shoulder as foll: bind off from each shoulder edge 7 (8, 8) sts twice, 8 (8, 9) sts once.

BACK

With smaller needles and MC, cast on 92 (98, 104) sts. Work in k1, p1 rib for 1½"/4cm. Change to larger needles and work in St st and MC only until piece measures 10½ (11, 11½)"/26.5 (28, 29)cm from beg, end with a WS row.

Neck opening

Next row (RS) Work 37 (40, 42) sts, join 2nd ball of yarn and work to end. Work both sides at once until same length as front to shoulders. Shape shoulders as for front. Bind off rem 15 (16, 17) sts each side for neck.

SLEEVES

With smaller needles and MC, cast on 60 (64, 68) sts. Work in k1, p1 rib for 1"/2.5cm. Change to larger needles and CC and work in St st for 2 rows.

Change to MC and cont in St st, inc 1
st each end every 4th row twice—64
(68, 72) sts. Work even until piece
measures 2½"/6.5cm from beg, end
with a WS row.

Cap shaping

Bind off 6 (6, 7) sts at beg of next 2
rows. Dec 1 st each side every other
row 11 (13, 14) times. Bind off 2 sts at
beg of next 6 rows. Bind off rem 18 sts.

FINISHING

Block pieces to measurements. Sew
shoulder seams. Set in sleeves. Sew
side and sleeve seams. With RS facing
and crochet hook, work 2 rows of sc
evenly around back opening, and work
two ch-3 buttonloops on 2nd row at top
of right edge.

1/2 Collar

With smaller needles and MC, cast on
23 (25, 27) sts. Work in k1, p1 rib for 3¾
(4¼, 4¾)"/9.5 (10.5, 12)cm. Bind off in rib.
With CC, pick up and k 54 (58, 62) sts
along one short and one long edge. P 1
row. With MC, k 1 row. Then work in rib
for 3 rows. Bind off in rib. Work other
half to correspond. Sew in place. Sew
on buttons.

CARDIGAN

LEFT FRONT

With smaller needles and MC, cast on
59 (62, 65) sts. Beg with k1 (p1, k1) at
beg of RS rows, work in k1, p1 rib for
1½"/4cm, end with a WS row. Change
to larger needles.
Next row (RS) K to last 6 sts, [p1, k1]
3 times (front band). Cont in St st,
keeping 6 sts at front edge in rib as
estabished, until piece measures 6½ (7,
7½)"/16.5 (17.5, 19)cm, end with a WS
row. Work 2 rows MC, 2 rows CC.

Beg chart

Next row (RS) Work 0 (3, 6) sts MC,
work 20st chart rep twice, work first 13
sts of chart once more, work 6 sts in
rib with MC.

Cont in pats as established until 12 rows of chart have been worked, then work 2 rows MC and 2 rows CC. Piece measures approx measures 8½ (9, 9½)"/21.5 (23, 24)cm from beg. Change to MC and work as foll:

Armhole shaping
Next row (RS) Bind off 5 (5, 6) sts (armhole edge), work to end. Cont to bind off from armhole edge 3 sts once, then dec 1 st every other row 6 (6, 7) times—45 (48, 49) sts. Work even until piece measures 12 (13, 14)"/30.5 (33.5, 36)cm, end with a WS row.

Neck and shoulder shaping
Next row (RS) Work to last 6 sts, place these sts on a holder.
Next row (WS) Bind off 9 sts (neck edge), p to end. Dec 1 st at neck edge every other row 6 times, AT SAME TIME, when armhole measures 5 (5½, 6)"/12.5 (14, 15.5)cm, bind off from shoulder edge (beg of RS rows) 8 (9, 9) sts twice, 8 (9, 10) sts once.
Place marker on front edge for 7 buttons, the first one ½"/1.5cm from lower edge and the last one 2"/5cm below neck and 5 others spaced evenly between.

RIGHT FRONT
Work to correspond to left front, reversing all shaping and working buttonholes opposite markers as foll:
Buttonhole row (RS) Work 2 sts, bind off next 2 sts, work to end. On next row, cast on 2 sts over bound off sts. Reverse chart pat as foll:
Next row (RS) Work 6 sts rib, work 20-st rep of chart twice then work first 13 sts once more, work 0 (3, 6) sts MC.

BACK
With smaller needles and MC, cast on 108 (116, 124) sts. Work in k1, p1 rib for 1½"/4cm, end with a WS row. Change to larger needles. Work in St st until same length as left front to armhole.

Armhole shaping
Bind off 5 (5, 6) sts at beg of next 2 rows, 3 sts at beg of next 2 rows. Dec 1 st each side every other row 6 (6, 7) times—80 (88, 92) sts. Work even until armhole measures 5 (5½, 6)"/12.5 (14, 15.5)cm.

Shoulder shaping
Bind off 8 (9, 9) sts at beg of next 4 rows, 8 (9, 10) sts at beg of next 2 rows. Bind off rem 32 (34, 36) sts for back neck.

SLEEVES
With smaller needles and MC, cast on 44 (48, 52) sts. Work in k1, p1 rib for 2"/5cm. Change to larger needles and CC and work 2 rows St st. Cont in St st with MC, inc 1 st each side every 4th row 11 (6, 2) times, every 6th row 3 (8, 12) times—72 (76, 80) sts. Work even until piece measures 9½ (10½, 11½)"/24 (26.5, 29)cm from beg, end with a WS row.

Cap shaping
Bind off 5 (5, 6) sts at beg of next 2 rows, 3 sts at beg of next 2 rows. Dec 1 st each side every other row 10 (12, 16) times, then *every* row 4 (4, 0) times, bind off 2 sts beg of next 6 rows. Bind off rem 16 (16, 18) sts.

FINISHING
Block pieces to measurements. Sew shoulder seams. Set in sleeves. Sew side and sleeve seams.

Neckband
With RS facing, smaller needles and MC, work rib across 6 sts of right front holder, with CC, pick up and k 73 (77, 81) sts evenly around neck edge, with 2nd ball of MC, work rib across 6 sts of left front holder. Work 1 row of rib matching colors. Cut CC and cont in rib with MC only for ¾"/2cm, making another buttonhole in right front band after ½"/1.5cm. Bind off in rib. Sew on buttons.

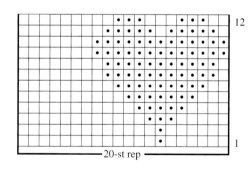

Color Key

☐ MC

▣ CC

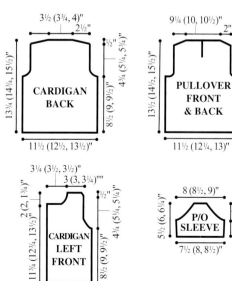

Lacy Stitch Layette

A thoughtful gift for a new baby: booties, bonnet, and a little sweater, all in a lacy stitch with ribbon trim. The light and lovely layette is cuddly soft in a delightful shade of green. The Lacy Stitch Layette first appeared in the Fall/Winter 1959 issue of the original *Vogue Knitting* magazine.

Lacy Stitch Layette

FOR INTERMEDIATE KNITTERS

SIZES
To fit 1 year.

KNITTED MEASUREMENTS
CARDIGAN
- Chest (closed) 21¾"/55.5cm.
- Length 10½"/26.5cm.
- Upper arm 7¼"/18.5cm.

MATERIALS
- 3 1¾oz/50g balls (each approx 203yds/187m) of Lang/Berocco *Bebe Lang* (wool 2) in #7174 green
- One pair size 3 (3mm) needles OR SIZE TO OBTAIN GAUGE
- 1yd/1m of ¼"/6mm-wide satin ribbon
- 3yds/3m of ½"/13mm-wide satin ribbon
- Stitch markers and holders

GAUGE
28 sts and 44 rows to 4"/10cm over St st using size 3 (3mm) needles.
FOR PERFECT FIT, TAKE TIME TO CHECK GAUGE.

STITCH GLOSSARY
Lace Pattern
(multiple of 6 sts + 3)
Row 1 (RS) K2, *yo, SKP, k1, k2tog, yo, k1; rep from *, end k2.
Rows 2 and 4 Purl.
Row 3 K3, *yo, SK2P, yo, k3; rep from * to end.
Rep rows 1-4 for lace pat.

CARDIGAN

BACK
Cast on 69 sts. Work in St st for 5 rows. K next row on WS for turning ridge. Cont in St st for 6 rows more. Work in lace pat until piece measures 6"/15.5cm above turning ridge, end with a pat row 4. Cut yarn and place sts on holder.

LEFT FRONT
Cast on 37 sts. Work in St st for 5 rows.
Next row (WS) Cast on 10 sts for border, k to end (turning ridge).
Next row K41, sl 1, k5.
Next row Purl. Rep last 2 rows twice more. Work in lace pat, ending row 1 as foll: K4, sl 1, k5; and ending row 3 as foll: K5, sl 1, k5. Cont as established until piece measures 6"/15.5cm above turning ridge, end with a pat row 4. Cut yarn and place sts on holder.

RIGHT FRONT
Work to correspond to left front, reversing pat and shaping.

SLEEVES
Cast on 51 sts. Work in St st for 5 rows. K next row on WS for turning ridge. Cont in St st for 6 rows more. Work in lace pat until piece measures 6½"/16.5cm above turning ridge, end with a pat row 4. Cut yarn and place sts on holder.

YOKE
Sl sts from holders onto needle, work next row from RS, as foll: left front, sleeve, back, sleeve, right front—265 sts.

Raglan armholes and neck shaping
Row 1 (RS) K5, sl 1, k4, yo, SKP, k1, k2tog, yo, k30, k2tog, pm, k2tog, k47, k2tog, pm, k2tog, k65, k2tog, pm, k2tog, k47, k2tog, pm, k2tog, k30, yo, SKP, k1, k2tog, yo, k4, sl 1, k5.
Row 2 Purl.
Row 3 K5, sl 1, k5, yo, SK2P, yo, k30, k2tog twice, k45, k2tog twice, k63, k2tog twice, k45, k2tog twice, k30, yo, SK2P, yo, k5, sl 1, k5.
Row 4 Purl. Cont in this way to dec 8 sts every other row 20 times more, AT SAME TIME, when armhole measures 3½"/9cm, shape neck as foll:
Next row (RS) Bind off 6 sts, work to end.
Next row Bind off 6 sts, work 11 sts and place them on holder, work to last 11 sts and place these 11 sts on holder. Cont to bind off 2 sts at beg of next 8 rows— 39 sts. Sl these sts to holder.

FINISHING
Sew side and sleeve seams. Fold hems at lower edge of body and sleeves to WS at turning ridge and sew in place. Fold hem at front edges to WS at sl st edge and sew in place.

Neckband
With RS facing, pick up and k 79 sts

around neck edge, including sts on holders. Work in St st for 5 rows. P next row on RS for turning ridge. Work 5 rows more. Bind off. Fold hem to WS at turning ridge, leaving ends open, and sew in place. Run ribbon through neck hem.

BONNET

Beg at front edge, cast on 75 sts. Work in St st for 5 rows. K next row on WS for turning ridge. Cont in St st for 6 more rows. Work in lace until piece measures 5¼"/13.5cm above turning ridge, end with a pat row 3. Cont in St st as foll: bind off 25 sts at beg of next 2 rows. Work even on rem 25 sts until side edge is same length as bound-off edge. Sl sts to holder.

FINISHING
Block piece. Sew side edges of back piece to bound-off sts. Fold front hem to WS at turning ridge and sew in place.

Front band
Work as for neckband on cardigan. Run ribbon through neck hem.

BOOTIES

Cast on 33 sts. Work in St st for 5 rows. K 1 row on WS for turning ridge. Cont in St st for 6 more rows. Work in lace pat until piece measures 2¼"/5.5cm above turning ridge, end with a pat row 4. Discontinue pat and work in St st as foll:

Instep
K11 and place sts on holder, k to end. Cut yarn and place last 11 sts on holder. Join yarn and work even on center 11 sts for 2"/5cm. Cut yarn.

Sole
Join yarn, and with RS facing, k 11 sts from holder, pick up and k 12 sts along side of instep piece, k 11 sts of instep, pick up and k 12 sts along other side of instep, k 11 sts from other holder—57 sts. Work even for 5 more rows.

Toe shaping
Next row (RS) K23, k2tog, k7, SSK, k23. P 1 row. Cont to dec in this way every other row, having 1 st less between dec on each dec row, until all center sts have been decreased. Bind off.

FINISHING
Block pieces. Sew sole and back seam. Turn hem to WS at turning ridge and sew in place. Run ribbon through the yo sts.

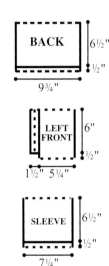

Scarves & Shawls

Shawls and wraps from decades
ago look up to the minute paired with
modern ensembles. Included are all
types of styles with something to suit
every taste, season, and occasion.

Photo: Fred Baker

This mohair and silk stole, backed with a contrasting fabric, exudes a sophisticated air of glamour. Ideal for evening wear, the elegant wrap is surprisingly simple and quick to knit. Shown in one size. The Easy Stockinette Wrap first appeared in the Spring/Summer 1951 issue of the original *Vogue Knitting* magazine.

Easy Stockinette Wrap

VERY EASY VERY VOGUE

SIZES
One size.

KNITTED MEASUREMENTS
● Width 20"/51cm.
● Length 72"/183cm.

MATERIALS
● 15 1¾oz/50g balls (each approx 73yds/67m) of K1C2, LLC *Truffles* (rayon 3) in #100 snow (A)
● 5 .80oz/25g balls (each approx 225yds/205m) of *Douceur et Soie* (mohair/silk 3) in #100 snow (B)
● One pair size 5 (3.75mm) needles OR SIZE TO OBTAIN GAUGE
● 2¼yds/2.1m contrasting fabric for lining
● Sewing thread for lining

GAUGE
20 sts and 28 rows to 4"/10cm over St st using size 5 (3.75mm) needles. TO SAVE TIME, TAKE TIME TO CHECK GAUGE.

Notes
1 Work with a strand of A and B held tog throughout.
2 K the first and last st on every row as a selvage st.

STOLE
Cast on 99 sts. Work in St st, working the first and last st as a k1 selvage st, until piece measures 72"/183cm from beg. Bind off all sts.

FINISHING
Block piece to measurements. Cut lining to fit stole plus ½"/1cm all around. Press under ½"/1cm for seam allowance. Slipstitch to all edges.

Photo: Lionel Kazan

This versatile lace and cable wrap can go effortlessly from casual to busines to evening. Make it with or without fringe in a color that suits your mood, and wardrobe. The Lace Wrap first appeared in the Spring/Summer 1960 issue of the original *Vogue Knitting* magazine.

Lace Wrap

VERY EASY VERY VOGUE

SIZES
One size.

KNITTED MEASUREMENTS
30" x 70"/76cm x 178cm.

MATERIALS
● 14 1¾oz/50g balls (each approx 137yds/125m) of Tahki•Stacy Charles, Inc. *501* (wool 3) in #219 beige
● One pair size 9 (5.5mm) needles OR SIZE TO OBTAIN GAUGE
● Cable needle (cn)

Note
The original color used for this shawl is no longer available. A comparable color substitution has been made, which is available at the time of printing.

GAUGE
31 sts and 24 rows to 8" x 4"/20cm x 10cm over 31-st rep of chart using size 9 (5.5mm) needles. TO SAVE TIME, TAKE TIME TO CHECK GAUGE.

STITCH GLOSSARY
8-st Front Cable
Sl 4 sts to cn and hold to *front*, k4, k4 from cn. Twist cable every 10th row.

WRAP
Cast on 136 sts.

Border row 1 (RS) *K1, p1; rep from * to end.
Border row 2 (WS) *P1, k1; rep from * to end. Rep border rows 1 and 2 twice.

Beg chart
Row 1 (RS) K1, p1, beg with st 1, work to rep, work 31-st rep 4 times, end k1, p1.
Row 2 and all WS rows P1, k1, p132 sts, p1, k1. Cont in pat as established, work cable twists on chart row 3 and then every 10th row thereafter. Work even until piece measures 69"/175cm from beg (or desired length), end with a WS row. Rep 2 border rows 3 times. Bind off 136 sts. Block piece.

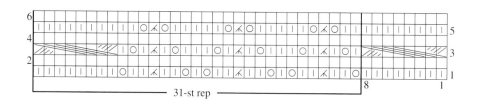

31-st rep

Stitch Key

☐ K on RS, p on WS

☐ P on RS, k on WS

Ⓞ Yarn over

☒ SK2P

▨▨ 8-st FC (twisted every 10th row)

Shield yourself from cool summer breezes with a wonderful, warm-weather shawl. Spectacular for seaside wear, it's wildly fringed with horizontal stripes in stunning shades of blue, gold, and white. The Striped Shawl first appeared in the Spring/Summer 1963 issue of the original *Vogue Knitting* magazine.

Striped Shawl

Photo: Leombruno-Bodi

VERY EASY VERY VOGUE

SIZES
One size.

KNITTED MEASUREMENTS
● 40" x 60"/101.5 x 152cm.

MATERIALS
● 11 1¾oz/50g balls (each approx 70yds/64m) of Classic Elite Yarns *Newport* (cotton) in #2092 blue (A)
● 10 balls in #2016 white (B)
● 3 balls in #2068 gold (C)
● One pair size 9 (5.5mm) needles OR SIZE TO OBTAIN GAUGE
● Size H/8 (5.0mm) crochet hook

GAUGE
18 sts and 24 rows to 4"/10cm over St st using size 9 (5.5mm) needles. TO SAVE TIME, TAKE TIME TO CHECK GAUGE.

STITCH GLOSSARY
Stripe Pattern
*10 rows A, 6 rows B, 2 rows C, 4 rows B, 2 rows C, 6 rows B; rep from * (30 rows) for stripe pat.

SHAWL
With A, cast on 271 sts. Work in St st and stripe pat for 60 rows. Dec 1 st each side of next row, then every 4th row 14 times more, then every other row 21 times—199 sts. Bind off 2 sts at beg of next 44 rows, then 4 sts at beg of next 16 rows. Bind off rem 47 sts.

FINISHING
Block piece to measurements. With RS facing, crochet hook and A, work 1 row sc evenly around all edges. For fringe, cut yarn in 16"/40.5cm lengths and place around shawl,) as shown in photo.

Scarves are the ideal project for busy, on-the-go knitters. Ever-decreasing ribs create interesting mitered ends on this Asian-inspired scarf, cornered with exquisite rose quartz decorative beads. The Geometric Scarf first appeared in the 1947 issue of the original *Vogue Knitting* magazine.

Geometric Scarf

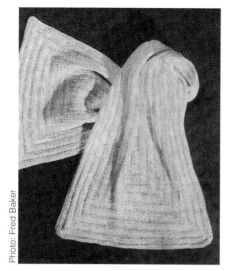

Photo: Fred Baker

VERY EASY VERY VOGUE

SIZES
One size.

KNITTED MEASUREMENTS
Approx 10" x 36"/25.5cm x 91.5cm.

MATERIALS
● 3 1¾oz/50g hanks (each approx 176yds/158m) of Koigu Wool Designs *Premium Merino* (wool 2) in #2231 pink
● One pair size 4 (3.5mm) needles or size to obtain gauge
● Four decorative rose quartz beads
● Sewing needle and matching thread

GAUGE
28 sts and 36 rows to 4"/10cm over k2, p2 rib (slightly stretched and blocked) using size 4 (3.5mm) needles.
TO SAVE TIME, TAKE TIME TO CHECK GAUGE.

STITCH GLOSSARY
Horizontal Rib
Row 1 (RS) Knit.
Row 2 Purl.
Row 3 Knit.
Row 4 Knit.
Row 5 Purl.
Row 6 Knit.
Rep rows 1-6 for horizontal rib.

SCARF
Cast on 70 sts.
Work 6 rows horizontal rib.
Rows 7 and 9 P2, cont horizontal rib to last 2 sts, p2.
Row 8 K2, cont horizontal rib to last 2 sts, k2.
Rows 10 and 12 K2, p2, cont horizontal rib to last 4 sts, p2, k2.
Row 11 P2, k2, cont horizontal rib to last 4 sts, k2, p2.
Rows 13 and 15 P2, k2, p2, cont horizontal rib to last 6 sts, p2, k2, p2.
Row 14 K2, p2, k2, cont horizontal rib to last 6 sts, k2, p2, k2.
Cont in pat as established, working 2 sts more in k2, p2 rib every 3rd row until all sts are in rib. Work in k2, p2 rib until piece measures 31½"/80cm from beg, end with a RS row.
Next row (WS) Work 32 sts in k2, p2 rib, p6, rib to end.
Next 2 rows K the knit sts and p the purl sts.
Row 4 Rib 30 sts, k10, rib to end.
Next 2 rows K the knit sts and p the purl sts.
Cont as established, working 4 sts more in horizontal rib at center every 3rd row until all sts are in horizontal rib and end of scarf corresponds with beg. Bind off.

FINISHING
Block scarf. Attach a bead to each corner.

This fun-to-stitch crocheted shawl is quick and easy to make. Rectangular with alternating petal motifs, it makes a sleek, sophisticated cover-up for warm-weather months. The Crocheted Wrap first appeared in the Spring/Summer 1954 issue of the original *Vogue Knitting* magazine.

Crocheted Wrap

VERY EASY VERY VOGUE

SIZES
One size.

CROCHETED MEASUREMENTS
32"x 72"/81cm x 183cm.

MATERIALS
Original Yarn
● 12 1¾oz/50g balls (each approx 110yds/100m) of Plymouth *Cleo* (cotton 4) in #371 dusty pink
Substitute Yarn
11 1¾oz/50g balls (each approx 120yds/112m) of Lily® *Sugar 'n Cream Sport* (cotton 4) in #20 French rose
● Size F/5 (4mm) crochet hook OR SIZE TO OBTAIN GAUGE

Note
The original yarn used for this shawl is no longer available. A comparable substitution has been made, which is available at the time of printing. Check gauge of substitute yarns very carefully before beginning.

GAUGE
8 petals to 6"/15cm over petal pat with size F/5 (4mm) hook. TO SAVE TIME, TAKE TIME TO CHECK GAUGE.

STITCH GLOSSARY
Petal Pat
Foundation Ch 4.

Petal Yo, draw up a lp in 4th ch from hook, yo and through 2 lps (2 lps left on hook), yo, draw up a lp in 4th ch again, [yo and through 2 loops] 3 times.

WRAP
Row 1 Ch 5, work petal; *ch 4, work petal; rep from * until there are 43 petals, piece measures approx 32"/81cm wide. Turn at the end of this and all following rows.
Row 2 Ch 7, work petal in 4th ch from hook, sc between first and 2nd petals of row below, *ch 4, work petal, sc between next 2 petals of row below; rep from *, end ch 4, work petal, dc to first ch of row below.
Row 3 Ch 7, work petal in 4th ch from hook, ch 4, work petal, skip 2 petals, sc to row below, *[ch 4, work petal] twice, skip 2 petals, sc to row below; rep from *, end ch 4, work petal, dc to ch sp of row below. Rep row 3 until piece measures 71½"/181.5cm from beg. Work row 2. Fasten off.

FINISHING
Join yarn to corner and work along side edge as foll: 3 sc in ch-7 sp, 2 sc in sp between petals. Fasten off. Rep along 2nd side edge. Block piece.

Photo: Sante Forlano

Embrace the outdoors with this incredibly warm and eye-catching plaid stole. Knit in luxurious cashmere/silk blend yarns and edged with fringe, this stole looks especially stunning worn over a pantsuit or jumper. The Plaid Stole first appeared in the Fall/Winter 1958 issue of the original *Vogue Knitting* magazine.

Plaid Stole

VERY EASY VERY VOGUE

KNITTED MEASUREMENTS
60" x 36"/152cm x 91.5cm.

MATERIALS
● 9 1⅞oz/50gm balls (each approx 145yds/132m) of Knit One Crochet Too® *Richesse et Soie* (cashmere/silk 2) each in #9510 green (A) #9841 ecru (B)
● Standard gauge knitting machine
● Crochet hook size C/2 (2.5mm)

GAUGE
28 sts and 44 rows to 4"/10cm at 5 with automatic guide. TO SAVE TIME, TAKE TIME TO CHECK GAUGE.

STOLE
Using 3 separate balls of yarn for each square, cast on 42 sts B, 42 sts A, 42 sts B—126 sts. *K 66 rows. Then reverse colors and k for 66 rows more; rep from * until there are 10 squares in length. Make another strip as above. Join in center with crochet sl st, reversing blocks (6 squares across and 10 squares down). With RS facing, using matching colors, work 1 row sc around all edges to prevent curling.

FINISHING
Block to measurements. With B, cut 10"/25.5cm fringe. With 8 or 4 strands, fringe both short ends of the stole.

Wrap up in style…this elegant two-toned knitted stole offers quick-to-knit glamour for all skill levels. Gorgeous over a sleeveless dress or gown, the cool dupioni silk lining feels luxurious against the skin. The Silk-Lined Stole first appeared in the Fall/Winter 1960 issue of the original *Vogue Knitting* magazine.

Silk-Lined Stole

VERY EASY VERY VOGUE

SIZES
One size.

KNITTED MEASUREMENTS
● Approx 21" x 70"/53.5cm x 177.5cm (blocked).

MATERIALS
● 5 1¾oz/50g balls (each approx 143yds/130m) of Schoeller Esslinger/Skacel *Merino Soft* (wool 3) each in #6 beige (A) and #12 red (B)
● One pair size 6 (4mm) needles OR SIZE TO OBTAIN GAUGE
● Size F/5 (4mm) crochet hook
● Lining fabric
● Sewing needle and matching thread

GAUGE
24 sts and 32 rows to 4"/10cm over pat st using size 6 (4mm) needles. TO SAVE TIME, TAKE TIME TO CHECK GAUGE.

STITCH GLOSSARY
Pattern Stitch (multiple of 4 sts + 3)
Row 1 (RS) With B, *k3, sl 1 wyib; rep from *, end k3.
Row 2 With B, *p3, sl 1 wyif; rep from *, end p3.
Row 3 With A, sl 1 wyib, k3; rep from *, end k2.
Row 4 With A, p2, *sl 1 wyif, p3; rep from *, end sl 1.
Row 5 With B, k1, *sl 1 wyib, k3; rep from *, end k1.
Row 6 With B, p1, *sl 1 wyif, p3; rep from *, end p1.
Row 7 With A, k2, *sl 1 wyib, k3; rep from *, end sl 1.
Row 8 With A, *sl 1 wyif, p3; rep from *, end p2.
Rep rows 1-8 for pat st.

STOLE
With A, cast on 127 sts. P 1 row on WS. Work in pat st until piece measures 70"/177.5cm. Bind off with A.

FINISHING
Block stole. With RS facing, crochet hook and A, work 1 row of sc around all edges, working 3 sc in each corner.

Lining
Using stole as a pattern, cut lining from fabric, adding 2"/5cm on all sides. With WS tog, baste stole and lining tog, allowing a 2"/5cm border on all edges. Turn under a ⅝"/1.5cm hem on fabric to WS and whip-st to RS of stole, mitering the corners.

Accessories

Vogue Knitting's accessory
designs are perennial in their
classic style and timeless appeal.
Included are his and hers basics,
from traditional argyle socks to
fashionable cabled gloves.

Photo: Fred Baker

A wardrobe basic—ribbed socks for men, women, and children, knit in go-with-everything neutral shades for years of easy wear. If desired, reinforce the heels and toes for added durability. The socks can also be easily lengthened to make knee-hi's. The Family Socks first appeared in the Summer 1955 issue of the original *Vogue Knitting* magazine.

Family Socks

FOR INTERMEDIATE KNITTERS

SIZES
Men's 9½ to 12.
Women's 8½ to 10½.
Children's 4 to 8 yrs.

MATERIALS
● 2 1¾oz/50g balls (each approx 238yds/220m) of Stahl Wolle/Tahki• Stacy Charles, Inc. *Socka* (cotton/wool/ polyamide 1) in #6120 green (child's)
● 2 balls in #0122 blue (woman's)
● 2 balls in #6124 dk blue (man's)
● One set (4) size 1 (2.25mm) dpn
● Stitch markers

GAUGE
36 sts and 44 rnds to 4"/10cm over k4, p2 rib (slightly stretched) using size 1 (2.25mm) needles. FOR PERFECT FIT, TAKE TIME TO CHECK GAUGE.

MAN'S SOCKS

CUFF
Cast on 64 sts loosely and divide evenly over 3 needles. Join, taking care not to twist sts. Place marker for end of rnd and sl marker every rnd. Work in k1, p1 rib for 3"/7.5cm, inc 8 sts evenly spaced across last rnd—72 sts.

LEG
Rnd 1 P1, *k4, p2; rep from * around,

end k4, p1. Place a 2nd marker center back. Rep rnd 1 for pat and work even until piece measures 6"/15cm from beg of leg.
Next rnd Work to last 23 sts of end of rnd, sl these sts and first 17 sts of rnd to 1 needle for heel, sl rem 32 sts on 2 needles for instep.

HEEL
K across heel sts, dec 4 sts evenly spaced across—36 sts.
Next row (WS) Sl 1 purlwise, p to end.
Next row *Wyib sl 1 purlwise, k1; rep from * to end. Rep last 2 rows 18 times more.

Turn heel
Next row (WS) Sl 1, p 20, p2tog, p1, turn. Sl 1, k7, SSK, k1, turn. Sl 1, p8, p2tog, p1, turn. Cont to work towards sides of heel, having 1 more st before dec on each row until 22 sts rem.

GUSSET AND FOOT
With same needle, pick up and k 18 sts on side of heel; keeping pat as established, work 32 instep sts to *Needle 2*; with *Needle 3,* pick up and k 18 sts on other side of heel and k 11 heel sts to same needle. Place markers for end of rnd and center of sole. There are 29 sts on each of *Needles 1 and 3*, 32 sts on 2nd, or instep needle. Work 1 rnd even.
Next rnd K to last 3 sts of *Needle 1,* k2tog, k1; work even across *Needle 2*;

on *Needle 3,* k1, SSK, k to end. Rep last 2 rnds 8 times more—72 sts. Work even in pat until 2"/5cm less than desired finished length.

TOE
Discontinue pat. Beg at center of sole, place 18 sts on each of *Needles 3 and 1,* and 36 sts on instep needle.
Rnd 1 K to last 3 sts of *Needle 1,* k2tog, k1; on *Needle 2,* k1, SSK, k to last 3 sts, k2tog, k1; on *Needle 3,* k1, SSK, k to end. K 1 rnd. Rep last 2 rnds until 20 sts rem. K5 sts of *Needle 1,* sl on *Needle 3* (sole sts).

FINISHING
Block. Divide sts onto 2 needles and weave tog using Kitchener st.

CHILD'S SOCKS

CUFF
Cast on 56 sts loosely, divide over 3 needles. Join, taking care not to twist sts. Place marker for end of rnd and sl marker every rnd. Work in k1, p1 rib for 1½"/4cm.

LEG
Rnd 1 *K3, p1; rep from * around. Rep rnd 1 until 4"/10cm from beg of leg, end 12 sts before end of last rnd. Sl last 12 sts and first 15 sts of rnd to 1 needle for heel; sl rem 29 sts to 2 needles for instep.

HEEL

K across heel sts, dec 1 st at center.
Next row (WS) Sl first st purlwise, p
to end.
Next row *Wyib sl 1 purlwise, k1; rep
from * to end. Rep last 2 rows 13
times more.

Turn heel

Next row (WS) Sl 1, p14, p2tog, p1,
turn. Sl 1, k5, SSK, k1, turn. Sl 1, p6,
p2tog, p1, turn. Sl 1, k7, SSK, k1, turn. Sl
1, p8. P2tog, p1, turn. Cont to work
towards sides of heel, having 1 st more
before dec on each row, until 16 sts rem,
end with a RS row.

GUSSET AND FOOT

With same needle, pick up and k 15
sts on side of heel, work 29 instep
sts to same needle, with *Needle 2*,
pick up and k 15 sts on other side
of heel, k first 8 heel sts to same
needle. Place marker for end of rnd
and center of sole (23 sts on *Needles
1 and 3*, 29 sts on 2nd or instep
needle). Work 1 rnd even, working
pat over instep sts.
Next rnd K to last 3 sts of *Needle 1*,
k2tog, k1; work in pat across *Needle 2*;
on *Needle 3* k1, SSK, k to end. Rep
last 2 rnds until 14 sts rem on each of
Needles 1 and 3—57 sts. Work even
until 1½"/4cm less than desired finished
length. Discontinue pat. K 1 rnd, dec 1
st in center of *Needle 2*.

TOE

Beg at center of sole, k to last 3 sts of
Needle 1, k2tog, k1; on *Needle 2*, k1,
SSK, k to last 3 sts, k2tog, k1; on *Needle
3*, k1, SSK, k to end. K 1 rnd. Rep last 2
rnds until 16 sts rem. K4 sts of *Needle 1*,
sl on *Needle 3* (sole sts).

FINISHING

Block. See man's finishing.

WOMAN'S SOCKS

CUFF

Cast on 66 sts loosely and divide on 3
needles. Join, taking care not to twist sts.

Place marker for end of rnd and sl marker
every rnd. Work in k1, p1 rib for 2"/5cm.

LEG

Rnd 1 K2, *p2, k4; rep from * around.
Rep rnd 1 for pat until piece measures
3"/7.5cm from beg of leg. Work next 32
sts to 2 needles for instep, k rem 34 sts
on one needle for heel, dec 2 sts evenly
spaced across heel sts.

HEEL

Row 1 (WS) Sl 1 purlwise, p to end.
Row 2 *Wyib sl 1 purlwise, k1; rep from
* to end. Rep last 2 rows 14 times more.

Turn heel

Next row (WS) Sl 1, p18, p2tog, p1,
turn. Sl 1, k7, SSK, k1, turn. Sl 1, p8,
p2tog, p1, turn. Sl 1, k9, SSK, k1, turn. Sl
1, p10, p2tog, p1, turn. Cont to work
toward sides of heel, having 1 st more
before dec on each row, until 20 sts rem.

GUSSET AND FOOT

With same needle, pick up and k 16
sts on side edge of heel; with *Needle
2*, cont in pat on 32 instep sts; with
Needle 3, pick up and k 16 sts on
other side of heel, k10 heel sts to same
needle. Place marker for end of rnd
and center of sole (26 sts on each of
Needles 1 and 3, 32 sts on 2nd, or
instep needle). Work 1 rnd, in pat
as established.
Next rnd K to last 3 sts of end of *Needle
1*, k2tog, k1; on *Needle 2* work across
instep sts; on *Needle 3*, k1, SSK, k to
end. Rep last 2 rnds 9 times more—64
sts. Cont to work in pat on instep sts
until 1¾"/4.5cm less than desired finished
length (16 sts on each of *Needles 1 and
3*, 32 sts on 2nd or instep needle).

TOE

Beg at center of sole, k to last 3 sts of
Needle 1, k2tog, k1; on *Needle 2*, k1,
SSK, k to last 3 sts, k2tog, k1; on *Needle
3*, k1, SSK, k to end. K 1 rnd. Rep last 2
rnds until 16 sts rem. K4 sts of *Needle 1*
and sl to *Needle 3*.

FINISHING

Block. See man's finishing.

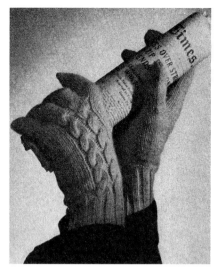

Cashmere is the ultimate luxury. Worked in a close-knit gauge on small needles, these gloves have long two-by-two ribbed cuffs and elastic inset cable panels for extra comfort. The Men's Cashmere Gloves first appeared in the 1948 issue of the original *Vogue Knitting* magazine.

Men's Cashmere Gloves

FOR INTERMEDIATE KNITTERS

SIZES
One size fits Adult's Medium (8"/20cm).

MATERIALS
- 2 1¾oz/50g balls (each approx 153yds/ 140m) of Filatura Di Crosa/ Tahki•Stacy Charles *Cashmere* (cashmere 4) in #73 grey
- 1 set (5) size 2 (2.5mm) dpn OR SIZE TO OBTAIN GAUGE
- Cable needle (cn)
- Stitch marker

GAUGE
26 sts and 40 rnds to 4"/10cm over St st using size 2 (2.5mm) needles. FOR PERFECT FIT, TAKE TIME TO CHECK GAUGE.

RIGHT GLOVE
Cast on 48 sts. Divide sts onto 3 needles as foll: 18 sts on *Needle 1*; 14 sts on *Needle 2*; 16 sts on *Needle 3*. Join, taking care not to twist sts on needles. Mark end of rnd and sl marker every rnd.
Rnd 1 *K2, p2; rep from * around. Cont in k2, p2 rib for 3"/7.5cm.

Beg pat and thumb gore
Rnd 1 K4, p1, k3, inc 1 st in next st, k1, p2, k1, inc 1 st in next st, k3, p1 (20 sts on *Needle 1* for back of hand); k6, inc 1 st in each of next 2 sts (for thumb gore),

k6 (16 sts on *Needle 2*); k16 sts on *Needle 3*—52 sts.
Rnd 2 K4, p1, k6, p2, k6, p1, k to end of rnd.
Rnd 3 Rep rnd 2.
Rnd 4 K4, p1, k6, p2, k6, p1; *k6, inc 1 st in next st, k to last 7 sts of *Needle 2*, inc 1 st in next st*, k to end of rnd—54 sts. Rep rnd 2 three times.
Rnd 8 K4, p1, sl next 3 sts to cn and hold to *back,* k next 3 sts, k3 from cn (6-st cable), p2, work 6-st cable, p1, rep between *'s of rnd 4 (for thumb gore) k to end—56 sts. Rep between *'s of rnd 4 for thumb gore every 4th rnd 5 times more and work 6-st cables every 8th rnd. There are 30 sts on *Needle 2* and a total of 66 sts after all incs. Work 1 rnd even.
Next rnd Work 27 sts, sl next 17 sts to contrast yarn strand for thumb and cast on 5 sts for inside edge of thumb, k to end—54 sts. Work even until hand measures 5"/12.5cm above ribbing, end with a cable rnd.
Next rnd Work to within 9 sts of end of rnd, sl next 14 sts to contrast yarn strand for little finger, cast on 2 sts over these sts—42 sts (for rem 3 fingers). Cont pat, work 4 rnds on the 42 sts. Discontinue cable pat.

Index finger
Next rnd K14 and sl to contrast yarn strand, k next 14 sts for index finger, sl rem 14 sts to other end of yarn strand and cast on 4 sts at end of finger—18 sts. Divide these sts on 3 needles and work in

rnds until finger measures 3"/7.5cm OR ¼"/.5cm less than desired length.
Dec rnd [K2tog, k1] 6 times—12 sts. K 1 rnd.
Dec rnd [K2tog] 6 times. Weave sts tog using Kitchener st.

Middle finger
Sl 7 sts of back of hand to dpn, k these sts and pick up and k 4 sts at base of index finger, k6 sts from palm of hand, cast on 3 sts at end—20 sts. Work in rnds until finger measures 3½"/9cm.
Dec rnd K2tog, k8, k2tog, k8—18 sts. K 1 rnd.
Dec rnd [K2tog, k1] 6 times—12 sts. Weave sts tog using Kitchener st.

Ring finger
Sl rem 15 sts onto dpn and divide onto 3 needles, picking up and k 3 sts at base of middle finger—18 sts. Work in rnds until finger measures 3¼"/8.5cm. Complete as for index finger.

Little finger
Sl 14 sts from yarn strand to dpn, picking up and k 2 sts at base of ring finger—16 sts. Work in rnds until finger measures 2½"/ 6.5cm.
Dec rnd [K2tog, k2] 4 times—12 sts. K 1 rnd.
Dec rnd [K2tog, k1] 4 times—8 sts. Weave sts tog using Kitchener st.

Thumb
Place 17 sts of thumb onto 2 needles.

Rnd 1 K17, pick up and k 5 sts at base of thumb—22 sts. K 2 rnds.

Dec rnd K to last 5 sts, k2tog, k3. K 2 rnds.

Dec rnd K to last 4 sts, k2tog, k2—20 sts. Divide sts onto 3 needles and work in rnds until thumb measures 2¾"/7cm. Complete as for middle finger.

LEFT GLOVE

Cast on 48 sts. Divide 16 sts onto each of 3 needles, pm at beg of rnd and work in rnds of k2, p2 rib for 3"/7.5cm.

Beg pat and thumb gore

Rnd 1 *Needle 1*, K14, sl last 2 sts to 2nd needle; *Needle 2*, K9, inc 1 st in each of next 2 sts, (for thumb gore), k3, sl last 4 sts to 3rd needle; *Needle 3*, K4, p1, k3, inc 1 st in next st, k1, p2, k1, inc 1 st in next st, k3, p1, sl last 2 sts to first needle, pm for new beg of rnd—52 sts. There are 16 sts on each of first 2 needles and 20 sts on 3rd needle for back of hand.

Rnd 2 K36, p1, k6, p2, k6, p1.

Rnd 3 Rep rnd 2.

Rnd 4 K16, k9, inc 1 st in next st, k to last 4 sts of *Needle 2*, inc 1 st in next st, k to end of rnd—54 sts. Work to correspond to right glove until there are a total of 66 sts after all incs. Work 1 rnd even.

Next rnd Work 26 sts, sl next 17 sts to contrast yarn strand for thumb and cast on 5 sts for inside edge thumb, work to end—54 sts. Work even until hand measures 5"/12.5cm above ribbing, end with a cable rnd.

Next rnd Work to within 1 st of end of rnd, sl next 14 sts to contrast yarn strand for little finger, cast on 2 sts over these sts—42 sts (for rem 3 fingers). Cont pat, work 4 rnds on the 42 sts. Then complete as for right glove.

FINISHING

Block pieces lightly, being sure not to flatten out ribs.

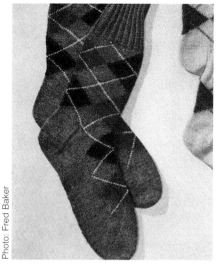

Photo: Fred Baker

Great Scot! With contrasting diamonds and diagonals, argyle socks have been a family favorite for decades. Knit the man in your life a pair of these bold basics and he'll treasure them for years. The Men's Argyle Socks first appeared in the 1947 issue of the original *Vogue Knitting* magazine.

Men's Argyle Socks

FOR INTERMEDIATE KNITTERS

SIZES
Size Medium (10½-11½).

MATERIALS
- 2 1¾oz/50g balls (each approx 184yds/170m) of GGH/Muench Yarns *Merino Soft* (wool 2) in #29 navy (A)
- 1 ball each in #20 light green (B), #22 dark green (C), #28 turquoise (D) and #12 gold (E)
- Size 2 (2.5mm) needles OR SIZE TO OBTAIN GAUGE
- 1 set (4) size 2 (2.5mm) double pointed needles (dpn)
- Stitch marker and stitch holders
- Tapestry needle

Note
Some of the original colors used for the socks are no longer available. Comparable color substitutions have been made, which are available at the time of printing.

GAUGE
33 sts and 40 rows to 4"/10cm over St st and argyle pat foll chart using size 2 (2.5mm) needles. FOR PERFECT FIT, TAKE TIME TO CHECK GAUGE.

STITCH GLOSSARY
K2, P2 Rib (multiple of 4 sts + 2)
Row 1 (RS) K1 (selvage st), *k2, p2; rep from *, end k1 (selvage st).
Rep row 1 for k2, p2 rib.

Notes
1 Cast on and work sock back and forth in rows on two needles to toe. Then join and work in rnds while shaping toe.
2 Cross lines may be embroidered in duplicate stitch after socks are knit.

CUFF
Beg at top edge with size 2 (2.5mm) needles and A, cast on 70 sts. Work in k2, p2 rib for 4½"/11.5cm, inc 1 st on last row—71 sts. Cont to work k1 selvage sts at beg and end of row, and rem sts in St st foll argyle chart for pat for 34 rows. Then work 1 more argyle rep only reversing B and C diamonds through row 34. Sock measures 11½"/29cm from beg. Adjust length at this point if desired.

INSTEP
Next row (RS) With A, k2tog, k16 then sl these 17 sts to a holder for heel; cont in argyle pat on center 35 sts (alternating C and B diamonds as before); sl last 18 sts to a holder for heel.
Cont in argyle pat on 35 sts for instep for 2 pat reps (68 rows). Cut yarn and leave instep sts on spare needle.

HEEL
Next row (WS) Rejoin A and p17 heel sts then p18 sts from other side to join heel at center—35 sts.
Next row (RS) Sl 1, k to end.
Next row Sl 1, p to end.

Rep last 2 rows until there are 32 rows in heel.

Turn heel
Next row (WS) Sl 1, p18, p2tog, p1, turn.
Row 2 Sl 1, k4, SKP, k1, turn.
Row 3 Sl 1, p5, p2tog, p1, turn.
Row 4 Sl, k6, SKP, k1, turn. Cont to work in this way always having 1 more st before dec, and work SKP on RS rows or p2tog on WS rows, until there are 19 sts on heel needle. Cut yarn.

Shape gusset
With spare dpn and A, pick up and k 17 sts on right edge of heel, k10 sts of heel on same needle; with another dpn, k9 rem heel sts, then pick up and k 17 sts on left side of heel—53 sts. Working back and forth on these two needles in rows, work as foll with A:
Row 1 Purl.
Row 2 *Needle 1* K1, SKP, k to end; *Needle 2* k to last 3 sts, k2tog, k1. Rep last 2 rows until there are 35 heel sts.

FOOT
Sl 35 sts onto one needle and work even with A in St st until there are same number of rows as in instep. Foot measures approx 8½"/21.5cm or 2"/5cm less than desired length from back of heel to end of toe. Make adjustments in length at this point (be sure to adjust instep length to correspond).

Shape toe

Beg at center of sole (the 35 heels sts in A), place sts on three dpn as foll: *Needle 1* 18 heel sts; *Needle 2* work the 18th heel st from *Needle 1* tog with the first instep st, work 33 instep sts; *Needle 3* work last instep st tog with next heel st, then work rem 16 sts—there are 17 sts on *Needle 1;* 34 sts on *Needle 2;* and 17 sts on *Needle 3*—68 sts in total. Join, mark end of rnd and sl marker every rnd.

Rnd 1 Knit.

Rnd 2 *Needle 1* k to last 3 sts, k2tog, k1; *Needle 2* k1, SKP, k to last 3 sts, k2tog, k1; *Needle 3* k1, SKP, k to end. Rep these 2 rnds until 20 sts rem. Divide sts on two needles and weave tog using Kitchener stitch.

FINISHING

Block socks lightly. If desired, embroider cross lines in duplicate stitch foll chart. Sew back and instep seams.

Color key

■ Navy (A)
□ Lt. Green (B)
■ Dk. Green (C)
■ Turquoise (D)
□ Gold (E)

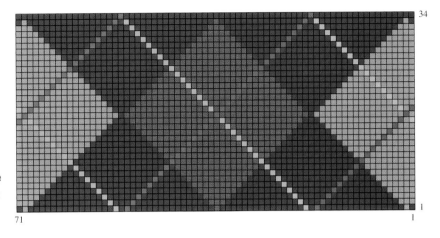

34

71   1   1

Photo: Fred Baker

Incredibly stylish wrist-length gloves are the perfect portable project. These elegant cabled gloves combine outdoor warmth with a sophisticated look ideal for all occasions. The Women's Cabled Gloves first appeared in the Fall/Winter 1951 issue of the original *Vogue Knitting* magazine

Women's Cabled Gloves

FOR INTERMEDIATE KNITTERS

SIZES
One size.

MATERIALS
● 2 1¾oz/50g balls (each approx 227yds/210m) of Schoeller Esslinger/ Skacel *Fortissima* (wool/nylon 1) in #6 red
● One set (4) size 1 (2.25mm) dpn OR SIZE TO OBTAIN GAUGE
● Stitch holders and marker

GAUGE
40 sts and 52 rnds to 4"/10cm over cable pat using size 1 (2.25mm) needles. FOR PERFECT FIT, TAKE TIME TO CHECK GAUGE.

STITCH GLOSSARY
Cable Pattern (multiple of 12 sts)
Rnd 1 *K2, p2, k6, p2; rep from * around.
Rnds 2 and 3 Rep rnd 1.
Rnd 4 *K2, p2, sl 3 sts to cn and hold to *back*, k3, k3 from cn, p2; rep from * around.
Rnds 5-12 Rep rnd 1.
Rep rnds 1-12 for cable pat.

RIGHT GLOVE
Beg at cuff, cast on 72 sts. Divide sts evenly over 3 needles. Join, taking care not to twist sts. Place marker for end of rnd and sl marker every rnd. Work in cable pat for 23 rnds.

Thumb gore
Inc rnd 1 K into front, back and front of first st (2 sts inc), k1 (4 gore sts), p2, work to end. Work 3 rnds even, keeping 4 gore sts as knit.
Inc rnd 2 Inc 1 st in first st, k1, inc 1 st in next st, k1, p2, work to end. Work 3 rnds even, keeping 6 gore sts as knit.
Inc rnd 3 Inc 1 st in first st, k3, inc 1 st in next st, k1, p2, work even to end. Cont to work in pat, inc 2 sts in gore every 4th rnd 5 times more, having 2 sts more between inc in each inc rnd—18 gore sts. Work even until 5 cable twists have been worked, end with pat rnd 4.
Next rnd Sl 18 gore sts on holder for thumb, cast on 2 sts, work across 70 sts—72 sts. Work even until 6 cable twists have been worked, end with pat rnd 12. Discontinue pat.
Next (dec) rnd *K6, k2tog; rep from * around—63 sts.

Index finger
K 11, sl next 44 sts to holder for other 3 fingers, on 2nd needle cast on 3 sts for gusset, k 8. Divide these 22 sts on 3 needles. K until finger measures 2½"/6.5cm.
Dec rnd 1 *K4, k2tog, k3, k2tog; rep from * once more—18 sts. K 1 rnd.
Dec rnd 2 *K3, k2tog, k2, k2tog; rep from * once more—14 sts. K 1 rnd.
Next rnd [K2tog] 7 times, cut yarn and draw end through rem 7 sts twice.

Middle finger
Sl next 8 sts from holder to needle, cast on 3 sts for gusset, sl 8 sts from other end of holder to free needle, k these 8 sts, pick up and k 3 sts over cast-on sts of gusset on first finger. Divide these 22 sts on 3 needles. Join and k in rnds for 2¾"/7cm. Complete as for first finger.

Ring finger
Sl next 7 sts from holder to needle, cast on 3 sts for gusset, sl 7 sts from other end of holder to free needle, k these 7 sts, pick up and k 3 sts over cast-on sts of gusset on second finger. Divide these 20 sts on 3 needles. Join and k in rnds for 2½"/6.5cm.

Dec rnd 1 *K3, k2tog; rep from * 3 times more—16 sts. K 1 rnd.
Dec rnd 2 *K2, k2tog; rep from * 3 times more—12 sts. K 1 rnd.
Next rnd [K2tog] 6 times. Cut yarn and complete as for first finger.

Little finger
Sl last 14 sts from holder to needle, pick up and k 3 sts over cast-on sts of gusset on third finger. Divide these 17 sts on 3 needles. K in rnds for 2"/5cm.
Dec rnd 1 K2, *k2tog, k1; rep from * 4 times more—12 sts. K 1 rnd.
Next rnd [K2tog] 6 times. Cut yarn and complete as for first finger.

Thumb
Sl 18 sts of thumb gore from holder to 2 needles, pick up and k 5 sts over 2 cast-on sts. Divide these 23 sts on 3 needles. K in rnds for 2"/5cm.
Dec rnd 1 *K3, k2tog; rep from * 3 times more, k1, k2tog—18 sts. Complete as for first finger.

LEFT GLOVE
Work as for right glove.

FINISHING
Block lightly.

Resources

Write to the yarn companies listed below for yarn purchasing and mail-order information.

AURORA YARNS
PO Box 3068
Moss Beach, CA 94038

BAABAJOES WOOL CO.
PO Box 260604
Lakewood, CO 80226

BARUFFA
distributed by Lane Borgosesia
PO Box 217
Colorado Springs, CO 80903

BERROCO, INC.
PO Box 367
14 Elmdale Road
Uxbridge, MA 01569

BROWN SHEEP CO.
100662 County Road 16
Mitchell, NE 69357

CLASSIC ELITE YARNS
300 Jackson Street, #5
Lowell, MA 01852

CLECKHEATON
distributed by Plymouth Yarns
PO Box 28
Bristol, PA 19007

DALE OF NORWAY, INC.
N16 W23390 Stoneridge Drive
Suite A
Waukesha, WI 53188

DESIGN SOURCE
PO Box 770
Medford, MA 02155

FILATURA DI CROSA
distributed by
Tahki•Stacy Charles, Inc.
8000 Cooper Ave.
Building #1
Glendale, NY 11385

GGH
distributed by Muench Yarns
285 Bel Marin Keys Blvd., Unit J
Novato, CA 94949

GARNSTUDIO
distributed by Aurora Yarns
PO Box 3068
Moss Beach, CA 94038

GRIGNASCO/JCA
distributed by JCA
35 Scales Lane
Townsend, MA 01469

JAEGER HANDKNITS
5 Northern Blvd.
Amherst, NH 03031
UK: Green Lane Mill
Holmfirth, West Yorkshire HD7 1RW

JCA
35 Scales Lane
Townsend, MA 01469

K1C2, LLC
2220 Eastman Ave, #105
Ventura, CA 93003

KOIGU WOOL DESIGNS
RR #1
Williamsford, ON NOH 2V0
Canada

LANE BORGOSESIA U.S.A.
PO Box 217
Colorado Springs, CO 80903

LANG
distributed by Berroco, Inc.
PO Box 367
14 Elmdale Road
Uxbridge, MA 01569

LILY®
PO Box 40
Listowel, ON N4W 3H3
Canada

MANOS DEL URUGUAY
distributed by
Design Source
PO Box 770
Medford, MA 02155

MUENCH YARNS
285 Bel Marin Keys Blvd., Unit J
Novato, CA 94949

NATURALLY
distributed by
S. R. Kertzer, Ltd.
105A Winges Road
Woodbridge, ON L4L 6C2
Canada

PATONS®
PO Box 40
Listowel, ON N4W 3H3
Canada

PLYMOUTH YARNS
PO Box 28
Bristol, PA 19007

REYNOLDS
distributed by JCA
35 Scales Lane
Townsend, MA 01469

ROWAN YARNS
5 Northern Blvd.
Amherst, NH 03031
UK: Green Lane Mill
Holmfirth, West Yorkshire HD7 1RW

SCHOELLER ESSLINGER
distributed by
Skacel Collection
PO Box 88110
Seattle, WA 98138-2110

SKACEL COLLECTION
PO Box 88110
Seattle, WA 98138-2110
UK: Spring Mill House
Baildon, Shipley
West Yorkshire BD17 6AD

STAHL WOLLE
distributed by
Tahki•Stacy Charles, Inc.
8000 Cooper Ave.
Glendale, NY 11385

S.R. KERTZER, LTD.
105A Winges Road
Woodbridge, ON L4L 6C2
Canada

TAHKI YARNS
distributed by
Tahki•Stacy Charles, Inc.
8000 Cooper Ave.
Building #1
Glendale, NY 11385

TAHKI•STACY CHARLES, INC.
8000 Cooper Ave.
Building #1
Glendale, NY 11385

WOOL PAK YARNS NZ
distributed by
Baabajoes Wool Co.
PO Box 260604
Lakewood, CO 80226

Vogue Knitting
233 Spring Street
New York, NY 10013
www.vogueknitting.com

We have made every effort to ensure the accuracy of the contents of this publication. We are not responsible for any human or typographical errors.

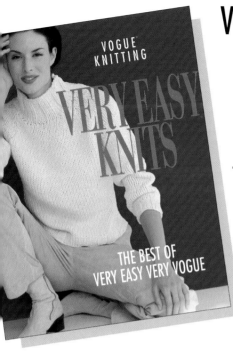
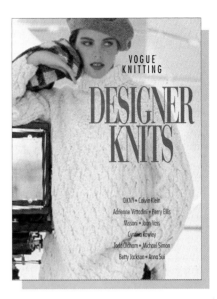

ACKNOWLEDGEMENTS

There are many people who contributed to the making of this book. In particular, and most importantly, we would like to thank all of the past and present editors of Vogue Knitting magazine for their vision and impeccable design selections. We would also like to extend our warmest appreciation and gratitude to all of the designers, knitters, and technical experts, whose combined skill and creative talents have enabled us to bring the best of knitting to our readers. Lastly, we would like to thank Michael Stier of Condé Nast Publications for his support and assistance in researching the vintage photographs.

PHOTO CREDITS

Paul Amato (pages 18, 33, 36, 51, 54, 72, 75, 78), Alan Cresto (page 48), Carlo Dalla Chiesa (page 39), Jack Deutsch (page 66), Tim Geaney (page 85), Torkil Gudnason (page 120), Greg Hinsdale (page 30), Barry Hollywood (page 21), Naomi Kaltman (page 94), Douglas Keeve (page 126), Brian Kraus (pages 98, 100, 102, 104, 107, 110, 113, 122, 124, 128 , 130, 133, 136, 138, 140), Francis Milon (page 118), Rudy Molacek (pages 12, 27), Peggy Sirota (page 88), Otto Stupakoff (page 60), Robert Trachtenberg (page 57), Charles Tracy (page 24), Nick Vaccaro (pages 15, 69), Tom Wool (pages 44, 63,82, 91).